TAROT PRIESTESS

About the Author

Leeza Robertson is the author of *Tarot Court Cards for Beginners* and *Tarot Reversals for Beginners*, and she's the creator of two tarot decks: the Mermaid Tarot and Animal Totem Tarot. When she doesn't have her nose inside a book or her fingers dancing across a deck of cards, she runs her online class with her business partner, Pamela Chen. Together they are the Head Witches at the High Vibe Tarot Academy, which you can find at bit.ly/uftamagic.

TAROT
PRIESTESS

Using the Cards to Heal, Grow & Serve

LEEZA ROBERTSON

Llewellyn Publications
Woodbury, Minnesota

FIRST EDITION
First Printing, 2022

Book design by Colleen McLaren
Cover image courtesy of Lo Scarabeo
Cover design by Cassie Willet
Interior art by Llewellyn art department

Llewellyn Publications is a registered trademark of Llewellyn Worldwide Ltd.

Library of Congress Cataloging-in-Publication Data
Names: Robertson, Leeza, author.
Title: Tarot priestess : using the cards to heal, grow & serve / Leeza Robertson.
Description: First edition. | Woodbury, Minnesota : Llewellyn Publications, 2022. | Summary: "A blend of tarot card meanings and a goddess-based spiritual path. Includes spreads, meditations, and exercises"— Provided by publisher.
Identifiers: LCCN 2022004501 (print) | LCCN 2022004502 (ebook) | ISBN 9780738765334 (paperback) | ISBN 9780738765488 (ebook)
Subjects: LCSH: Tarot. | Women priests.
Classification: LCC BF1879.T2 R61328 2022 (print) | LCC BF1879.T2 (ebook)
 | DDC 133.3/2424—dc23/eng/20220208
LC record available at https://lccn.loc.gov/2022004501
LC ebook record available at https://lccn.loc.gov/2022004502

Llewellyn Publications
A Division of Llewellyn Worldwide Ltd.
2143 Wooddale Drive
Woodbury, MN 55125-2989
www.llewellyn.com

Printed in the United States of America

Other Works by Leeza Robertson

Cirque du Tarot (Llewellyn, 2021)

Tarot Healer (Llewellyn, 2020)

Pathworking the Tarot (Llewellyn, 2019)

Animal Totem Tarot (Llewellyn, 2016)

Contents

INTRODUCTION

─────────)) ● ((─────────

Womxns' spirituality is a complex and oftentimes traumatic path. Throughout history, womxn's spiritual practices have been mocked and ridiculed and have oftentimes led to persecution and death. I am not just talking about cis womxn here either—I am including all who identify as womxn and all those who seek out feminine spiritual practices. You will notice that "womxn" is spelled in the inclusive manner, not the one given to us by patriarchy, the spelling that defines us as an addition to men. The goddess is not an addition, she is equal, her own whole being, sovereign. Which is why despite the danger, the call of the goddess comes to all who share her lineage, even though many fear the call and do not know how to serve her. For how does one step onto a path littered with so many wounds with an open heart and a devotional mind? Despite the efforts of the patriarchy to eliminate sacred feminine practices, we have seen a rise in womxn healing the devotional scar. From the Red Tent Movement to the Rise Sister Rise community to the swelling kundalini yoga community, the goddess is awakening and with her the call to service and leadership is being blasted out throughout the feminine world once again. *Tarot Priestess* taps into one of those rising paths, one that is also seeing a renaissance and calling all who identify as womxn from all over the world to come and serve at the feet of the goddess once again—the priestess.

I was initially introduced to the priestess in the nineties at university through my art history lectures; back then, these religious womxn were merely figures in a story. They belonged to a time that no longer existed, and history didn't seem to paint them in a very favorable light. Fast-forward to 2014 when I first set foot inside the Temple of Sekhmet not an hour from my home in Las Vegas, where I met a living modern-day priestess. I knew in that moment I was being called back to the goddess but didn't know how I was meant to serve her or what devotional practice looked like for me. It took me another three years to figure out that tarot was not only my priestess path, but also my way of serving the goddess. Never in my wildest dreams did I think there was a way to be a Tarot Priestess, but here we are more than twenty years from my initial invitation from the goddess and Tarot Priestess is exactly what I do.

What you are reading now is the pulling together of what I am calling the Tarot Priestess path. This book offers you another way to answer the call of these goddesses. You are invited to deepen your spiritual practices, heal devotional wounds, and rise in your own life as a daughter of the goddess. See yourself as a modern-day living priestess—a vessel of the sacred feminine, ready and able to serve in a way that is authentic to who you are while providing clues in answering the questions of why you are here in this life, in this body, and in this lineage.

Walking the Priestess Path

More than likely, you are already treading footsteps along your own priestess path and have been doing so for years without any conscious awareness of it. It's okay—I was also a walking spiritual zombie for a long time. I too was being guided by the goddess without truly recognizing it. I was carving out my own priestess path without any understanding of what I was doing, which is why I felt so compelled to write *Tarot Priestess*. I believe this book might just rub the sleep from your eyes and allow you to see what has always been right in front of you: your priestess self. If you have been using the tarot for spiritual practice or even incorporating it into some form of daily devotion and ritual, you are a Tarot Priestess. If you have ever called to the goddess pantheon and asked for help while placing a tarot card upon your altar while lighting a candle and saying a prayer, you are a Tarot Priestess. If you have used your tarot skills to help your larger community or take your tarot wisdom to conduct a sacred circle, used the cards in a form of healing, or even just used them for their designed divination purpose, you are a Tarot Priestess. The sacred act of selecting cards, asking questions of the Divine, and tapping into the universal consciousness for answers are all very priestess things to do.

If you are like me (also according to my guides) and are a little slow on the uptake, you just connected the dots between your tarot practice and one of the oldest feminine spiritual practices we have: the priestess. More than likely, you had or have a preconceived notion of what a priestess looks like and does on a regular basis. I know for me personally, the whole costume part was my biggest block. I have always had a perception that deeply spiritual practitioners looked a certain way, wore very specific clothes, and lived in some sort of religious, monastic way. It wasn't until I realized that this was me viewing feminine spirituality through the bullshit lens of the patriarchy that I was able to shift my perception. The old masculine rules of the Piscean Age have twisted and obscured our lens of femininity and feminine spirituality and how we express both. We have become so used to such narrow views of what it means to be feminine that it has become harder for us to truly identify when we are, in fact, in service to the goddess. The goddess comes in varying shapes, colors, sizes, abilities, and costume, which means if you dig around long enough, you will find one that looks, feels, and presents just like you do.

Womxn have for too long given away their power. It is now time to step up and reclaim that power, but not in a masculine way. It is important more than ever to awaken our priestess roles, bring our own feminine selves back to balance, and find out who we are and how we are meant to serve. Our communities need us—we have been hiding in the shadows for too long, and the masculine cannot play the feminine role. It has tried for a couple of thousand years and failed badly. We have to stop expecting the masculine to change and be something it is not. Instead, let us roll out of bed, put on whatever costume we damn well please, pick up our tarot cards, and offer ourselves to the goddess once again. If we womxn don't start putting ourselves back in positions of power, our lineage and spiritual practices will continue to erode, fade, and be desecrated until they are eventually lost forever. Writing *Tarot Priestess* is one step in the right direction; reading and using its content to deepen your own feminine spiritual practice is another. Sharing your own skills, magic, gifts, and self with your larger community is yet another step along the path of the Tarot Priestess.

Tarot as the Path, Initiation, and Temple

Tarot Priestess is structured to give you a framework to connect your tarot practice back to the goddess and recommit your feet to the priestess path. The chapters walk you through three priestess gateways and four goddess temples, and it also introduces you to the four stages of the initiation process. Some of the concepts within these pages may be new, especially if dancing with the goddess is unfamiliar to you. Or perhaps you may find the content reawakens your inner priestess and reminds her how confident and strong she felt when she was connected to a more conscious and structured practice. The tarot itself plays three very distinct roles in *Tarot Priestess*. The first is the path followed throughout the book's pages, guiding you through the gateways and the temples. When I use the word "path," I am referring to something we walk energetically, spiritually, emotionally, mentally, and physically. It might be one of the listed ways, or it might be all of them. The path is what takes us from one point to another, or in this case, through one lesson to another. The three gateways you will pass through are in the major arcana: these twenty-one cards have been broken up into three groups of seven to illustrate the roles each row of cards plays along the priestess path.

They are as follows:

- Gateway One, from the Magician to the Chariot: Ritual and Ceremony
- Gateway Two, from Strength to Temperance: Pilgrimage, Initiation, and Rites of Passage

- Gateway Three, from the Devil to the World:
  Reclaiming the Wild Shadow and Dancing in the
  Light

The second role the tarot will play in part two is the process of initiation, a process done via the court cards, as their built-in hierarchy is perfect for the many different levels to priestess training. Each court card has been assigned a position that one would hold within the temple. These positions give you a clear indication of how you will work your way up the initiation scale if this is what you choose to do. You do not have to work your way up, necessarily; a lot of people who enter spiritual studies find the position that is right and true for them and stay there. You started reading as one of these initiation personalities.

The stages of initiation are:

1. Neophyte/Page
2. Acolyte/Knight
3. Priestess/Queen
4. High Priestess/King

Perhaps you are the Page now, or maybe you are the Queen. You will find out as you make your way through the relevant chapters.

The last role the tarot will play is as temple—not a physical building but instead a temple framework. It is a sacred space of devotion, instruction, and connection. Your tarot deck will become the touchstone of your priestess work as well as the very vessel and space within which you will practice. The best part is that it is completely mobile, not tethered or restricted to one particular place. This allows for a sort of freedom in your spiritual practice to do it whenever and wherever you feel called, yet another form of breaking old stereotypes and creating new living models in which to align your new priestess identity. Instead of the priestess being tied to the physical location of the temple, your tarot deck becomes the priestess temple you can put in your pocket, place in your purse, or pack into your backpack and take wherever you go. Then again, you have already been doing this—you just didn't know you were carrying around an entire temple with you!

You will find the temples in the minor arcana, each providing you with an invitation to join the goddess and learn the skills and lessons of their respective temple through the corresponding suits. They are as follows:

- Temple of Pentacles: Connecting to earthly devotion with the daughters of Danu
- Temple of Swords: Truth, knowledge, and light with Saraswati
- Temple of Wands: Lighting your world on fire with Lilith
- Temple of Cups: Healing with the Lady of the Lake and the priestesses of Avalon

Due to the structured format, it is recommended you work your way through the content from cover to cover, at least initially. Each gateway leads to the next just as each temple lays the groundwork for the next. You can come back to work on just one gateway or dive deeper into one of the temples after you have read the information. Purpose, discipline, and organization are keys to your Tarot Priestess success, so consider this book your first lesson in ritual—you always start at a specific point and end at another.

The Role of the Fool

The cards of the major arcana show a journey: we start at the Magician and travel through the rest of the cards until we end up at the World. Throughout that journey, we grow, we are tested, we are broken, we are healed, and we are reborn. Each time we make this journey, we do so in the Fool's shoes. We may not always acknowledge this idea on a conscious level, but that doesn't make it any less true. The Fool puts on multiple hats and plays various roles each time we travel these twenty cards. In these pages and for this journey we are giving the Fool a very specific role to play and are doing so consciously—the Fool is us. We are dressing the Fool in a newly acquired priestess costume and slipping into the Fool's energy as we make our way through the three gateways of the majors. Your priestess costume will be different from mine and the costumes of other people who work with the content to come.

Your Fool will echo you and your journey, just as it does every time you pick up your cards. The only difference is that this time, you have given your Fool card a very specific role to play. Acting is second nature to the Fool, which is why it is easy for them to shapeshift and morph into any role we assign for them. The Fool is mutable and ready to embrace whatever shows up, quite excited to be on this new and deliberate priestess path with you. As you select your costume for the Fool, think about how you want to be seen as a priestess. What do these items of clothing mean to you? Maybe taking up robes and flowing gowns is something you get excited about. Or perhaps business casual is more your priestess attire. Just know that the costume you select for the Fool is the one you are the most comfortable wearing. It is the costume that makes you feel confident, strong, wise, and courageous. Clothing has the ability to change our mood, lift and elevate our energy, and allow us to tune in to our spiritual work in a more connected and focused way. Select your Fool's and your own outfit carefully.

Next, you will need to think about what tools you want to pack into the Fool's knapsack or bag. Although we don't normally know what the Fool has inside their wrapped collection of things, this time we are going to pack it with a few items that are relevant to us. If you include crystals in your daily devotion, you might want to think about packing a nice palm stone. If you write, throw in a pen and a journal. Obviously there will be a deck or two (or ten) of tarot cards in there as we are taking a journey as a Tarot Priestess, but which deck or decks will you pack for this journey? Which deck or decks speak with the loudest priestess voice? Next, you might consider some sage, salt, or palo santo sticks. Just remember not to make your knapsack too heavy—you do have to carry it on the rest of your journey; I dare say you will add to it as you make your way through the gateways and the temples. Make your selection—wisely or foolishly, the choice is yours alone to make.

Devotional Exercises

Throughout this book you will see various exercises just like this one. In these you will use your tarot cards in a hands-on practical way that brings your priestess work out of the world of theory and into the world of physicality. This is after all a tarot book, and tarot is a tactile tool. It is like having the entire wisdom of the goddess right in the palm of your hand. Each devotional exercise is designed to bring the learnings of each section together in a way that allows you to practice your priestess skills. Exercises might consist of, but not be limited to, a ritual, ceremony, spread, spell, altar work, and journal work. All of these activities will be done with your cards. I highly recommend selecting a deck or two to use with your priestess book. You might even wish to use one deck for the gateways and another for the temples. While I was putting together the exercises, I used multiple decks as I hunted for ones that suited the temples. I would use one deck for the wands, another for the cups, and so on. Just make sure that this deck or decks are not ones you will need to use for other readings, as you will more than likely want to leave the cards out as you work through the exercises. Let's jump right in, shall we?

For your very first exercise, you are going to need your tarot cards; I promise you do not need to make a commitment to the deck you grab for this exercise. You can change it to work with the gateways and temples. For now, just pick up the one within arm's reach.

Now you are going to see who you are as you start the priestess journey and what lessons and blessings are about to enter your life. Pick up your deck and hold it to your heart. Focus on your breathing, and feel the energy of your cards connect with your body. Ask the goddess to come to you now as you slowly close your eyes and hold the energy for a couple of breaths. When you feel attuned to the goddess's energy, shuffle your cards and draw.

CARD ONE: Who you are right now before you begin the Tarot Priestess journey.

CARD TWO: The blessing that is waiting for you on this new journey.

CARD THREE: The lesson the goddess wants you to learn on your journey.

Take your cards to your journal and spend some time with them before you move to part one.

Part One: The Gateways

Welcome to the gateways, your first stops along your priestess path. In this section of the book you will pass through three very important gateways before making your way to the temples of air, fire, water, and earth. Gateway one will introduce you to ritual and ceremony. These are important parts of your priestess practice. By walking through this gateway you will come to learn the difference between ritual and ceremony as well as when one may be used instead of the other. You may even learn that your entire life is made up of tiny rituals, small sacred acts that are constantly reinforcing the notion that you are already a priestess.

The next gateway you will pass through will introduce you to pilgrimage, initiation, and rites of passage. This is where you learn that oftentimes the act itself—the doing, the being, your life—is a pilgrimage that is part of your initiation. Don't be surprised if you get to the last page and realize that every hard knock and every joyful celebration was an important rite of passage along your priestess path. Just like with gateway one, you may end up being very surprised at how mundane and easily missed these important gateways are. You are passing through them every day, often without the awareness that they even exist or have shifted you in any way.

The third and final gateway you will dance through will assist you to reclaim your wild shadow self and bring your complete being into the light. One of the more important aspects of your priestess work will be connecting to the wildness within yourself and the physical world as well as in the spiritual ecstasy of movement. These concepts, which are often cast off as shadow work, are an integral part of the radiant work of the goddess. It is through these very acts that she shines through you, making you feel connected, complete, and alive.

The lessons within each of these gateways are fundamental to your priestess training. Being able to identify them, work with them, and possibly even explain them to others will be part of your own journey. You will have twenty guides for your travels in part one, so do not worry—you won't get lost or be left alone. Just follow the cards and let them lead, and you will be well on your way to sitting on the temple steps in no time.

Chapter One

GATEWAY ONE

From the Magician to the
Chariot: Ritual and Ceremony

〙 〉 ● 〈 〘

From the very first card, we are introduced to the concept of ritual. The Magician stands at a ceremonial table and could be said to appear as if in the middle of some magical ritual. This is often how one is introduced to the priestess path as well, through ritual and ceremony. It might be a celebration of a goddess, a circle to work with a particular phase of the moon, or even an event to herald in the changing of the seasons. These are all cultural rituals that a priestess may conduct or even participate in, events that often serve as our very first contact with priestess energy, just as the Magician is the first card of the Fool's journey in the major arcana.

The entire first row of the tarot takes us on a ritualist journey of our first encounters with the priestess path. Although it starts off rather exciting with the Magician, things get more serious as we move through these first seven cards. The next person we meet on our journey is the High Priestess herself, who lets us know that it is not the magical tricks of the physical world we are learning on this path; there is also a connection to a deeper, older, inner knowing. Mysteries that have drawn others like us to the feet of the priestess, time and time again.

The High Priestess instructs us on the deeper aspects of ceremony and how they are going to become a part of our daily life. From there, we move on to the Empress to learn how to bring nurturing rituals into our life and the lives of those around us. If we can't follow the priestess path for our own individual greater good, we won't be able to do it for the collective greater good. In many respects, the gateways are just this: steps in a larger living ceremony, starting with yourself and ending with the world. The gateways also help you create deep, meaningful practice for yourself so you can be an example to others. After all, isn't that how you found the path, watching some other priestess do what comes naturally to her?

The next card you will come across is the Emperor. This is where you learn how to build your personal practices. The Emperor will assist you to develop the skills and discipline to be confident in your priestess journey. The Emperor likes to be able to measure success, growth, and expansion. Be mindful of the lessons he has for you, as you may very well need them when it comes to seeing how well you are doing with your own spiritual work. I mean, there *is* a reason the next stop along your path is the Hierophant—when you first start your journey as a priestess, you need faith. More to the point, you need to be reminded why you are doing this work. Sometimes we can lose sight of why we have stepped onto this path and committed to this journey of service, surrender, and personal growth. The Hierophant is only too happy to assist and provide guidance on how to connect this work to personal devotion.

When who we are and what we do become one, life becomes a living prayer. A living ceremony and everything we do, from the moment our eyes open in the morning to when they close at night, becomes a sacred ritual. This is the lesson you were introduced to with the High Priestess. Here, the Hierophant gives you the next piece of the passage of the universal text. Or maybe it is only the next paragraph. Spiritual teachers don't ever give us too much to learn at once. My Buddhist teacher, Venerable Thubten Chodron, gives her teachings one line at a time so we can meditate on each word. This is the true meaning of practice, where even something as simple as reading becomes a ritualistic experience, and contemplation on each word is a single step in a larger ceremony. Once we have commenced with our instruction, it is time to find some like-minded friends, people who share a passion for the path we have chosen for ourselves. We might also know them as the Lovers.

Here on the Tarot Priestess journey, the Lovers isn't about romantic love (though I would argue it never is, but I digress). Instead, the Lovers can represent yourself and your need to connect with all sides of who you are and who you will become as you move further through the gateways. This card also marks another important ritual we all go through: finding someone who gets us, who is seen as compatible with the way we see the world. They could be our twin flame, those who can see our own heart and all its flaws and offer us a view of their own broken and repaired heart. This coming union helps solidify the rituals of compassion, communication, and vulnerability.

This need to belong to something bigger than ourselves is part of the driving force along the priestess path.

The last card you move through in the first gateway is the Chariot. This is where you take what you have learned so far and literally move with it. You speak aloud about newfound interests, sharing them with the world and making them part of your everyday life. In many respects, this is where we move out of the inner temple and into the outer one. By that I mean we shift our focus of ritual and ceremony as something intimate and solitary and take it into the larger community. You start to share the learnings of the priestess path or at least aspects of it with others. The Chariot drives this new movement and brings proof of momentum to your journey.

The lessons and devotional practices you will find in this chapter are all in alignment with the principles of this first gateway. Move through as the Fool archetype, full of wonder and anticipation for what is laid before you. Some of the devotional practices will speak to you more than others, but try the ones that feel the most uncomfortable, as they could be what unlocks the door to gateway two. Where there is resistance, there is a breakthrough just waiting to happen.

The Magician and the High Priestess

We learn about magic and the part we play in its co-creation right at the beginning of our Tarot Priestess journey, with the Magician and the High Priestess. The Magician introduces us to the tools of our new trade, and the High Priestess conducts our first initiation along this new path. When we first meet the Magician, she is in the middle of cleaning and resetting her altar. She tells you to come closer and invites you to help her as she starts to reposition the newly cleaned items. First she takes a chalice and puts some water in it, not quite filling to the top. She sprinkles rose petals into the water. While holding her hand over the top of the chalice, she mutters an incantation you can't quite make out. Then she dips two fingers of her right hand into the rose water and blesses herself. She motions for you to do the same.

Cautiously, you move toward her and follow her instructions. You feel the coolness of the water as you dip your fingers and then touch your third eye point, chin, and chest. The rose petals give off the gentlest of fragrances and calm you. The Magician takes the chalice and places it back on the altar. Next, she picks up a small dagger, holds the hilt in her right hand, and makes a slashing movement through the air. She explains to you that she is cutting away doubt and fear and turns the blade over to you, asking you to do the same. She explains that you need to think about the cords or ropes these fears or doubts have wrapped around you and visualize the dagger cutting them away, thus freeing you and making you able to move when Spirit calls.

You timidly make your own slashing movements, not really sure you are doing it correctly—after all, this is your first time at this sort of thing. When you feel you have done your cutting, you hand the dagger back and watch the Magician ever so gently place it to rest at the bottom of the chalice. Next, she picks up a gold coin. On one side of the coin is a pentacle. On the other is an engraving of a full moon framed by two crescent moons. The Magician explains to you this is the goddess's moon symbol and that the coin is used to remind us that the goddess always blesses us. She is giving and only wants all of her children to thrive. She then speaks a small prayer of thanks and gives the coin a kiss. She hands it to you and tells you to give thanks for your recent blessings, no matter how big or small. A few things come to mind and you speak them out loud, after which you kiss the coin and hand it back.

She places the coin at the feet of the goddess statue in the middle of the altar. Next, she picks up a wand that is intricately carved from wood and inlaid with crystals and silver. It is possibly the most beautiful wand you have ever laid eyes on. She holds the wand lengthwise and recites another incantation that you do not know or understand. She explains that the wand reminds us that we are all conduits of magic; the goddess's power runs through us, and we are each a powerful vessel of creation and manifestation. But first, she says, you have to believe that magic is real. You have to trust your connection to the goddess and have faith. She passes you the wand and asks you to hold it and silently say a prayer. She explains anything will do, even just the words "I believe" repeated over and over.

When you have finished your silent prayer, you hand the wand back and she places it at the feet of the goddess next to the golden coin. The Magician continues setting up the rest of her altar, placing more flowers and other objects as she hums to herself. The High Priestess walks towards you shuffling a deck of tarot cards.

"Now," she purrs, "let us see what lesson the goddess has for us this week." She stops shuffling and fans the cards out, asking you to select one. You look at the cards in the High Priestess's hands and close your eyes and take a nice deep breath as you steady yourself. For whatever reason, this seems like a big deal and you want to make sure you are focused, present, and aware in your selection. You reach out your hand and select one card. You turn it over and hand it back to the High Priestess. She smiles. "Good lesson. Thank you, Goddess," and hands the selected card to the Magician, who places it on its own stand on the now completed altar.

The High Priestess moves toward the altar and lights what looks like a small stick. She explains that sacred wood is burned to cleanse the energy of a space before beginning a prayer. The scent of the smoke is sweet and pleasant as she waves it over the now-complete altar. The Magician and the High Priestess take your hands and hold them as they begin a prayer. Although the words are in a language you have never heard before, you somehow feel the words deep in your core and the sound of the melodious prayer moves you. With their prayer finished, they drop their hands and place them into a prayer position, dipping their heads as they give thanks. They both smile at you and thank you for helping them to set their weekly altar.

"Please don't forget to drop by again," the High Priestess says as she moves to the back of the room. The Magician hands you a small stone and tells you to place this onto your own altar. She too walks away.

Devotional Exercise

I was brought up Catholic. Like most people who have a steady diet of religion at a young age, ceremony and ritual were introduced to me early in life. Although I was never too keen on church itself (what with all the kneeling and standing and kneeling again), the ceremony performance was always a pleasurable spectacle. Say what you want about the Catholic Church, but they know how to put on a show. Everything is rehearsed and staged right down to the final note of the final hymn. And the most decorated and primped place of all, the altar. I truly believe my need and love for altar space in my home and my spiritual practice comes from my Catholic upbringing. Granted, there were no tarot cards atop the glistening altar of my church, but the moment I found out that I could have a tarot altar, you bet I've had one ever since.

For this devotional exercise, you are asked to take a cue from the Magician and the High Priestess and create your very own tarot altar dedicated to your priestess journey. This altar will be a place for you to focus your priestess energy, perform daily rituals, and be the grounding place for any and all ceremonies you may choose to do throughout the year. Remember you will be displaying your tarot cards here, so you will need a place for them to stand upright without fear of them falling over. You can get as fancy or as simple as you like for your tarot card stand. I'm not the overly fancy type, so I tend to prop mine up against other items on my altar and hold them in place with crystals or whatever stones I may be using at the time. When it comes to selecting a card for your altar, you can do it intuitively if it is for your card of the day or even your card of the week or month. But a special ceremony will require you to choose your card deliberately and intentionally because you are building your altar around the energy of that card. Each card brings with it a unique story, vibration, and gift. Also keep in mind that you will need a special altar for your priestess work. You can keep it separate from your seasonal or healing altars, or you can make them all one and the same. The art of building an altar is a sacred and intimately personal practice. What is right for you will not be right for your priestess sisters. Know that whatever you decide is right and correct for you and your practice.

Here are some examples of different themes for your altar and the cards:

Seasonal Altar

Winter—Queen of Swords, Death, Three of Swords

Spring—Queen of Wands, the Empress, Ace of Wands

Summer—Queen of Cups, the Sun, Six of Cups

Fall—Queen of Pentacles, the World, Nine of Pentacles

Abundance/Prosperity Altar

To bring in money or money-making opportunities—Ace of Pentacles, Ace of Cups, Page of Pentacles

To grow your money or business—Seven of Pentacles, Knight of Pentacles

To give thanks for your financial blessings—Ten of Pentacles, Queen of Pentacles

To increase your financial position or a raise or promotion—Nine of Pentacles, King of Pentacles

Love and Romance Altar

To receive more love in your life—Ace of Cups, Page of Cups

Set the intention of meeting someone with whom you are soul-aligned—Two of Cups, Four of Wands, the Lovers

To spice up your sex life—Ace of Wands, Queen of Wands

To set an intention for a fun and flirty first date—Three of Cups

Protection Altar

To set a protection altar, any of the Knights will do. Here are a few examples of how they may be used.

To set boundaries around your home, finances, and body—Knight of Pentacles

To set boundaries and fortify your mind—Knight of Swords

To protect yourself from laziness or procrastination—Knight of Wands

To protect your heart and emotional well-being—Knight of Cups

These are just some ideas as to how to use your tarot cards to set the tone, hold the intention, and become the anchor for your sacred altar. I encourage you to write your own intention statements, prayers, or mantras to go with your cards so you can repeat them over and over again, as long as your altar is active. Once you are done with your altar, clean the space with sage or palo santo, put everything away, wipe your altar down completely, and if you want, change your altar cloth. Then it will be ready to be built again. There are no limits to how many altars you can have around your house at any given time, or how many times you can change your altar—all of that is up to you.

The Empress, Emperor, and Hierophant

Once you have an understanding of the tools at your disposal for your journey, it is now time to come to some understanding regarding the *why* and *why now*? Of all the things you could be doing, of all the roles you could be playing, why choose Tarot Priestess? In answering these questions, you will need instruction in how to use cycles, seasons, and nature as methods of time in the larger creation vortex. You will also need to learn how to build and maintain your priestess work as well as allow it to grow and support the community around you. Even though this one sounds tedious, you will need to learn the rules and regulations of this journey, as they will assist in helping you eliminate self-doubt and make you feel connected to something bigger than yourself. This path can be a solitary one, but it does not need to be a lonely one. For now, let us traverse the domains of the Empress, the Emperor, and the Hierophant. In many respects, these cards teach you how to instruct yourself, govern yourself, and (dare I say it) how to parent yourself.

Your next stop is the Empress. She invites you into her garden and asks you to come help her as she tends to a patch of newly grown vegetables. She beckons you closer and offers you a basket so you can load it up with fresh-grown items from around the garden.

"If you truly want to understand life," she says as she wipes the sweat from her brow, "grow a garden." Smiling, she returns to her crop and hands you produce as she picks, cuts, and pulls.

"Everything in this garden grows in its own time and in its own way. None of it can be rushed. And if the conditions are not right"—she shakes her head—"oftentimes things won't grow at all." She talks as if half to herself and half to you.

She gathers herself up and moves to another spot in the garden, indicating you should follow her. Once again, she kneels down and dives into her work. As she works, you take a closer look at the plants in the patch in front of you and notice that many of the leaves have been nibbled or seem to have bugs on them.

"I think you have a pest problem," you say to the Empress as you point to the plants you have been eyeing.

She laughs in response. "No, dear, those are not the calling cards of pests. Those are the markings of my fellow gardeners."

You look at her, bewildered.

"What you call bugs or pests, I call a necessary part of my garden. We all play a part in keeping this garden healthy, strong, and abundant. We need each other, even though we work separately."

"But don't they eat your crops and damage your plants?" you ask in genuine concern, thinking them to be nothing but miniature vandals and thieves stealing something that someone else has worked so hard to build and grow.

The Empress smiles and shakes her head. "Where you see destruction, I see yet another natural cycle playing out. Another dance of time, space, and co-creation."

As if on cue, a rabbit appears in the corner of the garden and starts to nibble on some of the lettuce growing in the patch closest to the gate.

"What is grown here is not just for me; it is for all those who need it. Creation in and of itself is never about us personally."

You look at her with a question sparkling in the corners of your eyes. "But don't we get something out of it? Isn't that why we do it in the first place?'

"Yes, of course—but for us, it is the work, challenge, and journey we so adore. The end result is just something that happens along the way, something made even more spectacular by sharing it with others."

The Empress stands up and dusts herself off, only managing to smear dirt all over her pants. She loads the last of the harvested produce into the basket and moves to yet another part of the garden, this time away from the vegetables. She stands next to a tree that has bright leaves and tiny tight buds.

"There is a cycle for all things; this tree's cycle is still in motion. Its buds are pregnant with possibility as it creates the conditions to bloom and fruit. But anything could happen between now and then. The nature of a cycle is unknown and never the same, no matter how many times it is repeated. However, this tree will go on creating until its own cycle has come to an end. During its life, it will create not for itself but for the birds, insects, and other living creatures that need what it provides."

She turns and looks deeply into you, almost as if she is seeing beyond your physical form—like she is seeing your soul.

"So what are you creating?" she asks.

She draws her hand up to halt a reply.

"Do not answer now. Instead, meditate on this question. Because like the tree, you are already pre-programmed to produce something that will be of great service to those who are drawn to you."

You do not dare reply, even when her hand is back down at her side and she is walking over to the other side of the garden. You quickly follow behind. She stops at what looks like a workshop. There are beautifully carved boxes and ornate birdhouses all over the place. So caught up in the beauty of the carvings are you that you don't see the Emperor approach until he is almost on top of you.

The Emperor motions for you to step into the workshop, though really looks more like a showroom. For a space that is filled with wood, woodworking machines, and tools of all sorts, it is remarkably clean. There is no dust to be found, and all the creations are on display as if in a museum. As if being able to read your mind, the Emperor asks, "Are you not proud of your creations?"

He spreads his arms and asks, "Do you not want to display them in the best possible way for all to see and appreciate them?"

"Come." He indicates a space next to a set of open French doors, where a lovely cool breeze is drifting over the worktable he seats you at. He hands you some sandpaper and a small birdhouse. It has a design of a ram carved into both sides and beautiful ornamental design work flows over the edges of the roof. Carved over the small opening is the most intricate crown you have ever seen.

"We put these in the garden for migratory birds over fall. Guests should always know they are welcome in our territory and I feel it is my responsibility to make sure they are comfortable and taken care of while they reside in my domain."

The Emperor points to your hand, which is holding the sandpaper. He motions for you to get to work. You start working the wood in front of you. The sandpaper is incredibly fine; the wood becomes soft and smooth under your fingers as you rub it. You notice as the Emperor picks up a piece of wood and begins to draw on it. You can see that he is mapping out another design. He is focused, controlled, as if everything else in the room has faded away, including you. He looks up and notices you staring at him. "Do you always spend so much time watching others work while you do nothing?"

You mumble something under your breath and go back to working on the little birdhouse, making sure to at least look like you are totally absorbed in the task at hand. Even though you have questions for the Emperor, you feel somewhat intimidated by his confidence, focus, and above all his discipline. Although a man of few words, the comments he has made hit home; you begin to start thinking about how you allow others to see or even find things you have created. Do you provide a safe and secure space for guests and visitors to your home? And how much time exactly do you spend looking at what other people are doing, when the time really could be spent on your own work, your own creations, your own life? You allow the act of sandpapering the birdhouse to become meditative as you ponder the few words the Emperor has spoken. You must have become lost in what you were doing because when you look up, you notice you are in the workshop alone. You get up, birdhouse in hand, and begin searching for the Emperor. The more you move around the workshop, the more incredible things you find: insect hotels, elaborate beehives, flower boxes, and the most intricate of seed feeders. It is as if the Emperor has single-handedly made enough houses and food containers for a small city of insects and wildlife. You hear voices on the far side of the workshop and you make your way toward them.

"Well, I see we have a visitor."

The Emperor's head turns your way and indicates for you to come join him and his companion. He introduces you. "This is the Hierophant. We were discussing the next blessing and laying ceremony of the feeders."

You nod your head like somehow you know exactly what they are talking about. The Hierophant gives a small laugh, as if feeling your slight confusion, and explains, "It is the way of the goddess that when we place things upon the earth, we ask her to bless them and take care of them so that those who need them can find them and benefit from them."

The Emperor nods in agreement. "At the beginning of each season, we replace the feeders, as different and new visitors will be coming by. We honor them by making sure they are taken care of. After all, it is partly our fault that they have a harder and harder time each year finding food and safe places to rest."

The Empress, who walked up behind you without you even noticing, adds, "We humans have spread far and wide, taking the land with us and bending it to our will. The goddess asks us to restore the balance, to give back what we can where we can."

"Everything here on this planet is only here for a brief moment, " says the Hierophant as they spread their hands. "We must honor that time by making it as easy as possible for those with whom we share that time. It is the goddess's will."

For the first time since you entered the workshop, you find yourself the center of attention, though you are not entirely sure if they are waiting for you to respond or if you are meant to indicate you understand. You hand the birdhouse back to the Emperor and nod your head in an awkward sort of way. The Empress and the Hierophant grin and ask you to follow them out of the workshop. They lead you down a path to another part of the garden, though it looks more like a field.

"This is the wildflower meadow," the Hierophant says gently. "Here we do our best to replicate what would have been here before humans took the land to farm. I guess you could say we have given it back—to the animals and to the goddess."

The field seems to suddenly come alive: flowers begin swaying in the breeze, and all around you dragonflies, bees, and butterflies flit through the air. You even notice small movement closer to the ground, where you are pretty sure you saw a small rabbit chasing a field mouse. The Hierophant spreads their arms wide and raises their head to the sky, taking a deep breath. "This is our temple. This is where we pray, serve, give thanks, and ask for guidance."

The Empress takes your hands in her own and looks into your eyes. "Everything you need to know about yourself and your place in the world can be found in this field. Everything here is needed, everything plays a part, nothing is considered useless or unnecessary. You grow and bloom exactly as you are meant to."

She bends down, picks a handful of wildflowers, and gives them to you. "For your altar, as an offering to the goddess." You look at the flowers in your hand and say "thank you" out loud. But when you look up, you notice you stand in the field alone. You lift your face to the sky, let the breeze whisper in your ear, and breathe deeper than you ever have before.

Devotional Exercise

Remove the Empress, Emperor, and Hierophant from your tarot deck and place them on your priestess altar. Each of these cards represents a step in a process you are going to complete. The Empress asks you to find a way to use your skills to give back to those around you. Are you able to throw a dinner party for friends to honor the role they play in your life? Are you able to make something for the wildlife in your area and place it in your garden? Perhaps you can plant some trees or even more bee-friendly plants in your garden. Maybe you knit and can make hats and scarves for your local shelter and hospice. The Emperor reminds us that our gifts are not our own, that they are given to us for a reason, to share with our local community. As part of your priestess journey, you will need to get comfortable with sharing your skills with the world beyond your front door. The Hierophant reminds you this is a sacred act, a devotional act, to honor the goddess for her blessings, to honor yourself for how you are blessed, and lastly, to honor your community by allowing them to participate in your blessings. On a piece of paper, write what your gift to your community is going to be. Remember, it doesn't have to be people-based. It can be a gift to the earth or to the animals. Once you have your gift written out, place it in front of your tarot cards on your altar. You will also need a natural offering for the goddess, be it some flowers (wildflowers are best), a crystal or river rocks, some leaves, wood, and sand or even dirt. Ideally you have a pink candle for this ritual, but a white tea light will work just as well. Once your priestess altar is set up, light your candle, making sure it is far away from your cards and anything else that is flammable. Recite the following prayer:

> Dear mother Empress, divine creator, I offer you my skills and my service.
>
> Dear father Emperor, divine creator. I offer you my gift and ask that you direct me to where it is most needed.
>
> Dear uncle Hierophant, teacher and mentor, I offer you my faith; keep me focused on my task and do not allow me to waiver.
>
> With these offerings I give thanks to all that you have blessed me with.
>
> For it is in your blessings that I now confidently bless others in my life.
>
> You have taught me that when I show up and give of myself, expecting nothing in return, I am giving from my most divine aspect.
>
> Through your divinity, I am learning to find my own divine purpose.
>
> I give you these offerings humbly and from the heart.

> A gift to the land, a gift to my community, and a gift of faith.
>
> I honor you, divine creators, in all of your glorious splendor and infinite wisdom.
>
> And so it is.

Once you have spoken your prayer out loud, leave your candle burning if it is possible. If you can't, let it burn for five to ten minutes and recite the following before you blow your candle out:

> On extinguishing this flame, I let my prayer be carried on the breeze, knowing that you, Empress, have heard my prayer; that you, Emperor, are putting things into motion; and that you, Hierophant, are holding me steadfast in my faith. What is said is now done.

Leave your altar up for a minimum of twenty-four hours, seventy-two hours maximum. Pack all of your ritual items away and clean your altar before setting it up again.

The Lovers and the Chariot

You walk toward a small chapel to the left of the field where you have been picking wildflowers. Suddenly, you notice something sparkling as if catching the light. You watch as the light beams and dances around in this particular spot. You decide to walk over to it and check it out. Lying beneath the long grass and swaying flowers is a small compact mirror, which surprisingly is open and undamaged. Perhaps it fell out of someone's bag while they were having a picnic in the meadow. You imagine this would be an ideal spot for a picnic. You reach down and pick up the mirror. The case is silver and etched with the most intricate patterns; it is cool to the touch even though it has been lying exposed to the elements in the full sun. You run your fingers over the sides of the compact and slowly flip it over to see the back. On the bottom of the compact you see it has been engraved, perhaps with the owner's name. The engraving reads: *"To my one true life partner, now and forever ..."* and in bold writing you see your own name! You turn the compact over and look at it more closely, yet all you see is your face reflecting in the mirror. Your eyes linger on the reflection staring back at you. For whatever reason, you really take the time to look and see who is staring back. You gasp when you realize it is you, but not the you holding the mirror. The reflected version of you seems to be glowing, radiating with light. Mirror-you looks truly joyful, as if they don't have a worry in the world. The reflection smiles, and you can't help but smile back. How interesting to see yourself but know it's not the same version of who you are right now. Only you will know if it is a future you, a past you, or a version of you in another time and space.

You close the compact and put it in your pocket. Now you turn back toward the small chapel, running your fingers over the tops of the wildflowers as they dance in the midday breeze. As you get closer to the chapel, you notice there is a bicycle leaning up against the outside wall. It has a lovely wicker basket attached to the front. Loaded up inside the basket are the wildflowers the Empress gave you along with one of the birdhouses the Emperor built. You consider that perhaps the bicycle's owner is visiting the chapel with the Hierophant and head inside to see if you can find them. As you reach for the door, though, you notice it has a thick metal chain looped through the handles, held together with a substantial-looking padlock—

no one is going to cut through these anytime soon. There is no way anyone is inside the chapel. So what's up with the bike, you wonder. You move toward it, and as you get up on it, you notice it has a note stuck to the seat. You lift it off and read it. The note says: "Hope you like the wheels! The Empress calls it the chariot. Drive with care and let your heart be your compass. All our love, E, E & H." Mystery solved. The bike is yours. No more wandering around on your feet. It's time to upgrade your travel equipment.

Devotional Exercise—The Lovers

To begin this section, you will need to remove both your Lovers and Chariot cards from your deck. You are going to place your Lovers card on your bathroom mirror. If you don't like the idea of having one of your cards in the bathroom, photocopy it and place that on the mirror instead. This card is your reminder to look into the mirror daily, so place it somewhere that forces you to see yourself at eye level. Place next to your card a sticky note or piece of paper bearing the words "I am enough." Every time you wash your hands, clean your teeth, or do your hair or your face, you will see both the Lovers and your affirmation statement. Look yourself in the eyes as you repeat the affirmation out loud or inside your head (when cleaning your teeth!) for as long as you are standing in front of the mirror. The Lovers card is the anchor and connection to the goddess, a reminder that you are the ultimate gift of her divine love and because of this, you will always be enough. The Lovers is your physical and vibrational selves becoming one under the loving gaze of the mother, goddess energy. This is a simple but powerful ritual, one that has the potential to shift your thinking in very significant ways. Keep your card and sticky note on your bathroom mirror for as long as you feel it is necessary. You may even end up keeping it there as you get used to this bathroom ritual. As you continue this practice, you will notice the energy around you shift—it will be subtle at first, starting with you feeling a little less stressed and perhaps even a little more relaxed about life in general. But if you keep up with it daily, you will notice new experiences, opportunities, and possibilities come your way. Just know that not every new thing that crosses your path is right for you; make sure whatever new thing you encounter aligns with your desired direction. These new things must offer the opportunity to upgrade your ride in service of your priestess goal, whatever it may be.

Devotional Exercise–The Chariot

The thing about movement is that you need to know the direction you are headed. Sometimes you need a map to make sure you stay on track. Other times you need a compass. This spread is both map and compass, showing you information from all four directions—north, east, south, and west. This spread starts at the central point (where you are now) and will show you that what awaits you depends on what direction you decide to go.

To start this spread, remove your Chariot card from your deck and place it facing up in front of you. Then pick up the rest of your deck and give it a shuffle. Once you have shuffled, hold the deck to your heart, close your eyes, and take a few deep breaths. Connect with your cards and draw the first card. Place it on top of the Chariot. Now give the deck another shuffle and flip over the first four cards from the top of the deck and place them as illustrated below.

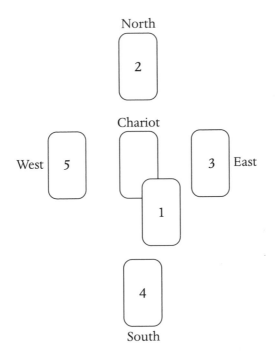

CARD ONE: The area of your life in which momentum is needed.

CARD TWO/NORTH: This is what awaits you if you move in the direction of your higher self. This is the lesson or gift your inner star will learn or receive.

CARD THREE/EAST: This is what awaits you if you decide to go with something new. It is a new way of moving or a new method of travel.

CARD FOUR/SOUTH: This is what is waiting for you if you choose to be playful and spontaneous.

CARD FIVE/WEST: This is what is in store for you if you follow the advice of others, especially those who have already traveled the path on which you now find yourself.

Do not be too hasty when choosing a direction to pull from—the more favorable cards may not necessarily get you the results you want. Sometimes learning a hard lesson means we won't have to repeat it further along the path. Think very carefully before you decide which direction to go. Spend some time journaling about your cards, and maybe even flip one last card over in the center to see what words of wisdom the goddess has for you about the journey you now find yourself on, the one of Tarot Priestess.

Chapter Two

Gateway Two

From Strength to Temperance: Pilgrimage, Initiation, and Rites of Passage

――――――――) ❭ ● ❬ (――――――――

In this chapter, you will traverse the second row of your Fool/ priestess journey. A lot happens in this row. Lessons come hard and fast as you move out into the external world, the world of experiences. It is little wonder that this row, your second gateway, begins with Strength; you will certainly need to be strong in the face of adversity and opposition. You will need to find your inner resilience and build your confidence. The lessons you learned in the first gateway will reappear and test you as you move through this one. All of this is part of your initiation as a priestess.

As you get your bearings here at the beginning of the second gateway, you notice something else: once again, you are alone. The path of personal pilgrimage has begun. This could be a physical act and/or an emotional one, but it is always spiritual. As you move from Strength to the Hermit, you also move from the light to the dark. The only light you will have for the next step of your journey will be the lamp the Hermit bestows upon you. This lamp will only light your way one step at a time, teaching you patience, trust, mindfulness, and pace. The act of pilgrimage is both a rite of passage and an initiation to see if your body, mind, emotions, and spirit can be attuned for greater purpose. This is your first test as a priestess.

The Hermit's lamp will ultimately lead you to the Wheel of Fate. You may also know it as the Wheel of Fortune, but a priestess knows that all circumstances are fortunate and that luck is merely a matter of perspective. For this reason, the goddess teaches us to look upon the Wheel instead as the inevitable turning of time, the change of seasons and the cycles we go through as a collective species. This broader understanding of the Wheel will change how you view the external world. As you will see, it is something that is playing its part, not something that can bend to your will or intend your personal harm. The Wheel reconnects you to the natural order: the cosmic rhythms of the world in which you live, dance, breathe, and worship. Everything is as it should be, all the time, without fail. As the Wheel turns and things change, so too does your experience.

How you perceive this natural order will be explored in the next card—all matters fair, just, and balanced are Justice's favorite. A priestess must learn that outcomes, situations, and even opportunities have an order to them; they are never about individuals but about the greater good. The ability to see beyond the self and look at the much larger picture is Justice's job. It is a lot harder than you think to be constantly keeping the balance in favor of the many and not just the few. The goddess wants as many of her children as possible to feel free, safe, and secure; Justice is only too happy to see the goddess's will be done.

Perhaps the relationship between the goddess and Justice is why the Hanged Man comes right after—once the goddess has her say, you have to surrender to her ruling. Letting go isn't the easiest thing for humans, but on the priestess path you will need to master this very important step. Think of it this way: when one walks the priestess path, they will need to know when to put their heart above their head and when to plant their feet on the ground and let logic and reason have their turn. The Hanged Man is a dual energy in this respect. Master this knowing and you will be sure to have your first awakening in the Death card.

Death marks a very important part of the path and the pilgrimage section of this book as a rite of passage and a new point of initiation. You meet this card as one version of yourself and leave it as another, reborn and ready to leave the surface journey you have been taking thus far, moving deeper into the spiritual part of your priestess training. Death is very much a two-part process: there is death itself—it may be death of the ego, of an old life, or an old belief system—and then there is the rising, resurrection, and rebirth. This time, you enter the world without ego as ruler, with a new life, way of seeing, moving, and believing in the world. As a priestess, you will need to be able to maneuver all parts of the death process. This means you will also need to know when to move from one step of the process to another. This rite of passage is not something you stay in; rather, you move through it so you can end up in the loving arms of Temperance.

Temperance is your soft landing place here at the end of the second row of the major arcana. She stands ready to heal and restore you, to get you aligned with your new energy and deal with any remaining wounds you may have after coming through the death process. In many respects, Temperance is the energy healer of the tarot, ready to lay hands on you and bring you back to yourself. In addition, she prepares you for the last row, the last gateway of your priestess journey. And trust me when I tell you that you will need all the healing energy you can get before dancing with the Devil.

Strength and the Hermit

You find your feet back on the path. It looks familiar, but only in a dreamscape kind of way as you know you have never physically been here before. Everything around you is strange and different, yet not all at the same time. You feel a pull deep inside you, a yearning to walk this path and learn its lessons and hear its story. It is as if this thing of compacted earth beneath your feet is a living thing that speaks to you as it pulses under your toes. However, you have no idea where this path goes or what will happen along the way, and you certainly don't feel as prepared as you did when you had the aid of the Chariot.

Fear blooms inside you, dragging doubt along with it. You question the direction your feet are facing and wonder ever so briefly if you should just turn around and head back to the safety of where you just came from, the known. But before your mind can catch up, you notice your feet are moving, taking you further and further away from where you first started. Resigned to the fact that you have already started, you keep walking, putting one unsure foot in front of the other. Still feeling the pull and being pushed along by the pulse, fear still unfolds … yet you must go forward. The call seems bigger and stronger than you and your resistance. Gravity now has you in its orbit, helpless to change course, and at the mercy of the energy that now guides your every movement. Swallowing hard, you dig deep to find whatever courage you have, place your hands in your pockets, tilt your head up, and march on.

The further you walk, the clearer the world around you becomes. The dream seems to be shifting, or maybe you are just merging into the dream. To be honest, it is hard to tell from your perspective. There is also no way to orient yourself as the landscape doesn't seem to show a clear, direct way to navigate due to its shifting nature. Like it or not, you have to surrender to the direction of the path, having no choice but to keep your eyes focused straight ahead. As you continue to make your way along the path, you notice a light off in the distance. At first you think it might be a star due to its position in relation to what you consider the horizon line. But as you keep moving, you soon realize it is on a hilltop.

The path winds its way through what appears to be a valley; not too far ahead, you see the path starts to move upward, as if toward a beacon. It would appear that you are headed in the direction of the starlike light. The path continues to wind its way gently up the slope of the hill. What you first thought was a star is in fact a large lamp hanging on an ornate wooden pole carved with intricate patterns. The lantern itself is decorated with a star etched into the glass. And hanging under the glass is an envelope that bears your name written in beautiful script. You turn it over and pop the seal, removing the letter carefully. It reads:

> *Welcome to the hermitage.*
>
> *This is a place of quiet contemplation and reflection. You will find great courage and strength during your stay,*

more than you ever thought possible. But that does not mean your stay will be easy.

Do not be surprised if during your stay you find your worst fears and deepest doubts dropping by to say hello.

We want you to know that the light that guided you to this point is also the light that will show you the way out of the darkness that is to come. We want you to find some way to become one with your shadow, with the parts of yourself that you often avoid. Here in the hermitage, there is nowhere to run or hide. Only when the answer you seek reveals itself will the next part of your journey be illuminated.

We wish you all the best.

S & H

Devotional Exercise–Strength

At this point on the priestess path, you may be starting to feel like the work you have stepped up to do is bigger than you are, which might make you feel less than strong. The good news is that this is exactly *how* you move from thinking about your own needs and wants and shift into thinking about how you can lead others. Your task right now isn't just about you, and you don't have to do it alone. The original Rider-Waite-Smith version of this card features a beautiful illustration of this idea; in it, the angel Ariel stops to assist the prideful lion. Even the most powerful amongst us need help, experience vulnerability, and require others in order to prosper.

At the beginning of your pilgrimage, you were asked to draw on your own strength. The cards will let you know if you are being asked to give help or ask for it. For this exercise, remove your Strength card from the deck. This is a three-card altar spread, so you will place these three cards on your altar and meditate with them over the next few days.

Once you have your Strength card faceup in front of you, pick up the rest of your deck and shuffle the cards. Pull one card from your deck and place it on the left side of your Strength card. This card will let you know if you need to ask for assistance or if you are doing pretty well right now. Shuffle your cards one more time and select one more card and place it to the right of your Strength card. This card will show if you are being asked to assist someone else and the suit will let you know in what capacity. If this card is a King, Queen, or major arcana card, you are being asked to share your strength and resilience in a leadership role. The card will provide you clues about how and where to do this.

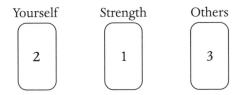

Yourself   Strength   Others

2   1   3

Once you have your cards drawn, pull out any additional tarot books you have and journal with them. Keep your journal work around the concepts discussed in this chapter so you have a focus. Next, place your cards on your altar and light the pink (or white) candle while you spend some time in meditation with this spread. Once you have finished your meditation, you can blow your candle out and light it again the next time you come to be with this spread. When you know your time is up with these cards (around the third to seventh day), place them back in your deck.

Devotional Exercise—The Hermit

Here in the Hermit we are working with the many parts of a pilgrimage: the way of the path, the way of the journey, the way you are taking this journey. We are working with who you are becoming along the path. For this exercise, remove your Hermit from your deck. Next, select two cards in your deck: one that represents who you are right now as you embark on your priestess pilgrimage and another for who you wish to be once you are done with your journey. Look through your cards, keeping all cards faceup. You will use both cards to pathwork, a process I wrote about in *Pathworking the Tarot*. In a nutshell, pathworking is a form of active meditation.

Here you will allow yourself to imagine / visualize / meditate on the journey you will need to take to become the future you. Use the cards you have selected to provide points of meditation. Focus mainly on the visuals of the cards you have selected. Really study the colors, poses, and feeling the image gives you. Let's just say you pulled one of the Pages to represent where you are and pulled a Queen to be who you wish to become. There are many things the Page will need to do in order to become Queen, including dressing differently, speaking differently, and engaging with people around them differently. Allow all of this to play out in your meditation, as if you are watching it as a movie. As a passive observer, stay in this space for as long as the movie takes.

Once you have completed your pathworking exercise, pick up your journal and start making notes about what you saw, heard, or learned about the journey you are taking. Do not try to make sense of the information pouring out of you right now. Just allow the words to flow down your arm and out of your pen. There will be time enough to make sense of it later. After you have completed your journal work, you can either keep your cards on your altar for further work or just put them back in your deck.

The Wheel and Justice

Pilgrimages are about taking a journey and movement, though not just in a physical sense. During your time at the hermitage, you would have noticed that you shifted, journeyed, and traveled spiritually, mentally, and emotionally. This type of inner pilgrimage is just as important as one taken with your physical feet; in many respects, the two go hand in hand. One will often precede the other in a cycle of initiation. Once you have done the inner work, it is time to put your feet back on the path and move to the next phase of your journey, one with the ability to spin any outcome into your life and your priestess training.

The Wheel of Fate / Fortune creates outer movement in your life, reminding you of the cycles you travel, seasons you grow and age with, and time that is constantly moving. Nothing on your path will stay the same for long, and the Wheel is here to remind you of that. It can bring a new beginning into your life or it can close a door. It can indicate the middle of a pilgrimage and might even forecast what energy you are moving into. Everything is moving, spinning, changing—and what a relief that is. How horrible would it be if a hard time could never end, if a cycle of darkness would never see the light? There is a natural law to the Wheel that blends perfectly with the karmic energy of Justice. Both cards deal with movement through balance.

Devotional Exercise

In many respects, the Wheel spins the path of your pilgrimage into being. When you come to the Wheel, you see your options illustrated on its surface. Each one will give you a different experience, possibly separate lessons, and maybe even a different outcome. You never can tell with fate. As we all do, you give the wheel a spin and a path is selected. It is neither good or bad, it is just the path you decide to walk. It may seem like a very random way of making decisions, but it makes just as much sense as letting the mind form pro and con lists. One could argue, however, that the Wheel is always being spun, that we never logically make any decisions about the direction we head in life. The Wheel of Fate is always directing where we are headed.

Perhaps the reason Justice comes right after this card in the Rider-Waite-Smith tarot is to remind us that all decisions made on the Wheel have karmic implications. Each path laid out in our lives allows us to elevate our karmic destiny. As Shakespeare said, all the world's a stage, and we are merely its players. The Fates have already written the script, and though the ending may not be set in stone, you get to bring your character to life in any way you choose. The Wheel has spun the priestess path into your life. Let us just say that it was fate that made you pick up this book, and part of your karmic destiny is to move yourself from being a seeker to a position of devotion.

For this spread, you will need two tarot decks: one will be the cards used to show you what fates or fortunes will be spinning into your life over the course of the seasons, and the second will show you how these are connected to karmic order and balance. I highly recommend using two decks that are very visually different, and you might even want to consider using one tarot deck and one oracle deck for this spread. Whatever you choose, make sure that the decks have cards that are named or are a match to either Justice or the Wheel.

Deck one: Remove your Wheel of Fortune card from that deck and place it faceup in front of you. Pick up the remaining deck and give it a shuffle. Hold the deck to your heart for a few breaths and open yourself up to connect with the goddess of fate and fortune. She may reveal herself as a word, a whisper, a touch on the cheek, or a flash of color behind your closed eyes. Once you feel her presence, draw your cards and place them in the following spread:

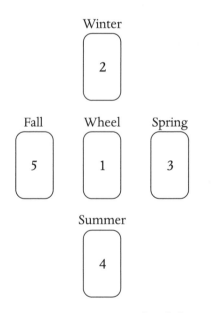

DECK TWO: Remove your Justice card and place it next to your Wheel of Fortune card in the center of your spread. Give your deck a shuffle and hold the cards to your heart. This time, call in the energy of Justice, the goddess of law, order, and balanced results. When you feel or know she is with you, go ahead and lay your cards in the exact same way as before, laying them just on top of the cards you pulled for the Wheel.

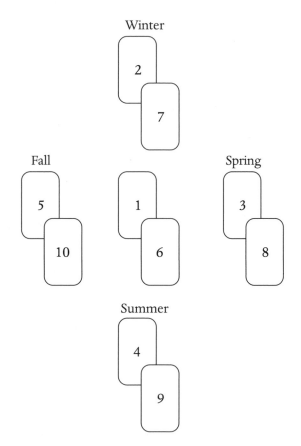

Winter

2

7

Fall

5

10

Spring

3

8

1

6

Summer

4

9

CARDS 1 AND 6: Your center cards are the driving energy of this spread; you may also call them your significator cards.

CARDS 2 AND 7–WINTER: These cards show you what is happening or possibly could happen come winter.

CARDS 3 AND 8–SPRING: These cards speak of energy spinning into your life come spring.

CARDS 4 AND 9–SUMMER: The heat of summer and its possible fate lay here.

CARDS 5 AND 10–FALL: The harvest energy is upon you in this position. What did you sow, and what karma will it restore?

Start reading this spread in the season you are currently living in. As I write, we are coming to the start of spring, so I am going to begin reading there. I then move around the spread and stop with winter. Reading your spread this way will give you the most accurate information to work with and show you where you might need to make some changes or what season you need to prepare for. This is a complex spread that is going to give you a lot to work through. Take your time. Do not rush it. Pull out all of your tarot books and dive deep into the cards and the story they are spinning into your life. You have been blessed by the guidance of two goddesses—do not squander it.

The Hanged Man

When walking the priestess path, surrender is an important lesson to learn. There is much about the act of surrender people misunderstand, mainly because they believe it means something will be taken away from them. However, the spiritual act of surrendering is about opening oneself up to receive everything. The human ego is limited; it cannot comprehend the vastness of the universe and therefore clings to control out of fear. Here in the Hanged Man, however, you are learning how to love, put your heart above your head, and experience true freedom.

The Hanged Man pats the spot next to him on the tree and invites you to sit, look around, and sway upside down in the breeze. Let go of expectations; free yourself of stress and pressure, and drop your attachment to ego-related outcomes. This is surrender. Swinging on a branch with the wind in your hair and the sun on your face reminds you of what it was like to be a child, full of wonder, awe, and curiosity. This is how you allow the goddess into your life: by coming to her as that curious child, ready to be filled with an abundance of miracles. So swing, let your arms go, drop the pressures and burdens you have been carrying on your shoulders, and be free.

Time on the Hanged Man's tree is limited. This is not a space you can stay in indefinitely. At some point, you will need to put your feet back on the ground. But for now, enjoy this feeling of liberation. Here on the Hanged Man's tree, nobody needs anything from you. No one makes any demands of you, and there are no expectations—it is just you, the tree, and the elements. There is no place to be and nowhere to go. This is a sacred space, one that offers itself to you as a gift. At some point, you will pass this gift on to another. As a Tarot Priestess, you will facilitate this space for others, playing the role of the Hanged Man to give people a place on the tree of surrender. For now, it is just yours. Close your eyes and absorb this feeling into the very cells of your body. File it into your memory and imprint it on your conscious mind. The more you can retain about this experience, the better it will be when your time in this space is over. Breathe in. Breathe out. Arms and fingers stretched wide. You are safe. You are free.

Devotional Exercise for the Hanged Man

By the time we arrive at the Hanged Man, we realize that some things on the path are out of our control, that there are some things we need to surrender to and let a higher power take care of. This is an exercise in opening the heart and trusting the way—of the path, of the journey, and how we are slowly becoming one with our priestess selves.

The best way to practice this surrender, this handing over of things beyond your control, is through ritual or prayer. Here is where you invoke the goddess, call her into your life, and let her handle things that seem too big or overwhelming and beyond your logical resolution. For this ritual you will need a pink candle to represent heart energy. You will also need to write what you are handing over to the goddess on a piece of paper, and also a picture of which goddess you will be working with. Recommended goddesses for this ritual are: White Tara, Mother Mary, Aphrodite, Hathor, and Aine. If you have a goddess you are familiar with who works with heart energy, by all means write her name.

Place all the items on your altar. You can place your request/petition inside a jar with some salt for protection, some rosemary for healing, a rose quartz for the heart, and your Hanged Man card. Secure your candle to the jar lid by melting some of the wax and sticking it on top of your jar. Placing all your items inside a jar is good for small altar spaces and those who wish to concentrate the energy of their prayer. That said, you do not need to place your items into a jar for this ritual; any way in which you feel guided to set up your altar is just fine.

Once you have everything set up and your candle is lit, repeat the following prayer/petition:

> Goddess, Goddess, see this light
>
> Goddess, Goddess, hear my plight
>
> Upon this altar I do declare
>
> All that I wish to spare
>
> Remove it now
>
> Remove it with ease
>
> Goddess, Goddess, release it from me
>
> With ego mind now asleep
>
> My heart beats strong with each gone thing
>
> Goddess, Goddess, heal it within me
>
> I open my arms, ready to receive
>
> Goddess, Goddess, lay your blessing on me
>
> I will walk your path
>
> And be your light
>
> Goddess, O Goddess, let this prayer take flight
>
> I release it now
>
> As above so below
>
> My prayer is done.

Once your prayer is complete, you can leave your candle burning as long as it is safe to do so. Otherwise, you can blow it out and do the prayer again until the candle has burned all the way down.

Death and Temperance

I remember the first time I walked a labyrinth as a spiritual act. It was 2012 and I had just read Rachel Pollack's *The Body of the Goddess*. I had driven to the local priestess temple here in Las Vegas, which has a labyrinth behind it. In the center is the silhouette of an ancient goddess. The idea is to enter the labyrinth with the intention of leaving something behind when you get to the center, then ask for healing as you walk your way back to the start. This is Death and Temperance in action: what you leave behind is what you offer for Death to take. It is something you are done with and you hand over to the goddess to turn back into vibrational energy so it can go back to the universe from which it came. This is something you will do many times on your priestess path—just as you will notice having multiple labyrinth experiences. Once you have made your offering, you honor it by healing, allowing Temperance to alchemize and rebalance your vibrational, emotional, and physical bodies. With each step you take away from the center of the labyrinth, the more healing you are meant to allow in.

I no longer remember what I first offered the goddess on that day of my labyrinth initiation; honestly, I was too concerned about screwing up the process! But since that day I have released beliefs, emotions, relationship hooks, and attachments that no longer serve me. What you hand over to the Death card will be personal and you are under no obligation to share it with anyone else. Just know that here in the last two cards of the second gateway, you are only halfway through your labyrinth experience (finished in the next gateway). I emphasize this as I do not want you to think that Temperance is your final stop—there is more work to do in the labyrinth.

For now, the goddess calls to you, asking you to search your heart for your offering. She wants you to be very sure of what it is you will hand over to the Death card. You stand at the opening of the labyrinth, head bowed, hands at your heart. Do not seek this answer with your head. Listen to the beat of your heart. Let it tell you what needs to stay with the goddess. Close your eyes, breathe. Only when you know what it is you are leaving behind, step onto the path and walk toward the song of death, rebirth, and healing.

Devotional Exercise

You do not need to stand at the mouth of a physical labyrinth to benefit from this part of the pilgrim's journey. Even though there is something deeply powerful in walking the steps inside the vortex a labyrinth creates, you can offer your gift to the Death card anywhere, at any time. It is just as powerful to close your eyes and imagine you are walking with the goddess, allowing her to guide your steps, surrendering to the pull of healing, and offering the Death card that which no longer serves you. You can do this as meditation, placing your Death and Temperance cards on your altar, or you can just close your eyes and let your mind wander to your inner labyrinth. How you decide to do this is totally up to you. Just know that no matter which way you get to your inner labyrinth, the goddess will be waiting for you. She will be there to instruct you on how to let go, how to surrender, and how to open up to be healed.

To prepare yourself for this part of your pilgrimage, remove your Death and Temperance cards from your tarot deck and place them faceup where you can see them. Get a notebook and a pen, and start listing things you wish to release inside the labyrinth. Select one that is weighing on you heavily. It might be a feeling, thought, old belief, situation, or even a relationship. Once you have selected your one thing to give to the Death card, write about how you will feel once this is no longer your energy to carry. Write it in as much detail as possible. Write about how your body, mind, and soul will feel once this energy is taken from you and how you will allow Temperance to heal and reset you once it has been given away.

When you are done writing, either close your eyes and start imagining or light a candle and place your cards on your altar and begin your meditation. Take as long as you need on this part of your journey. There is no rush and no wrong or right way to walk these steps. You may even have to come back to this exercise a couple of times before you feel you have finally released the energy of your offering completely. Once you have finished your imagining/meditation, return to your notebook and journal on any and all findings. Put it all on paper, as oftentimes the most insignificant thing is actually the key to the biggest transformational change. If you set your altar and lit a candle for this exercise, make sure you have a safe place for it to continue to burn or blow it out.

One final word about this part of your journey: this is just one piece of your priestess training. Do not linger here unnecessarily. Once you have made your one offering, let Temperance heal you and move on. Healing spaces are for healing work only, not for living in. Staying in a healing space too long will make it toxic and undo all the good work you have accomplished. We move in and out of these spaces for a reason; they serve a very specific purpose. Once that is completed we leave them. That is not to say you can't come back or will not need this space again—you will. This exercise is about understanding what a healing space is and is not. The labyrinth is a temporary space that you must leave to continue with the rest of your pilgrimage.

Chapter Three

Gateway Three

**From the Devil to the World: Reclaiming the Wild
Shadow and Dancing in the Light**

——————————— ❭❭ ● ❬❬ ———————————

In this chapter, you will move through the last row of the Fool's/
priestess journey. This can be a difficult row to get through. In
many respects, this row is your dark night of the soul: you may
struggle before you feel the freedom on offer with these cards.
You have to be plunged into the darkness before you can stand
in the light. There is shadow work to do here but probably
not the kind you have been taught before. This last row of the
major arcana is difficult, more so than the two before it. You
will need to be gentle, kind, and compassionate with yourself
as you move from the Devil to the World. You may feel things
you do not wish to, and you may resist the incredible liberation
that comes by completing this gateway. However, it will all be
worth it if you can stick with it and see the journey through.

The reason this row is more difficult than the others is that
you are working here to claim a part of yourself that may not
feel normal: the wild part of your soul. Rewilding is one of

many initiation processes. It is important, as it is part of infusing the unlimited potential of the goddess back into your daily experience. Raw power can scare people, especially when it is coming from a womxn. I have been teaching entrepreneurs long enough to know that power; how to wield it, claim it, and own it is a very difficult topic for some womxn, mainly because it is not taught. The patriarchy is set up to strip womxn of power, to see them as less than their male counterparts. They are not partners or equals and are therefore not allowed to be wild and untamed. It is quite astonishing to see how deeply this internalized narrative affects modern-day womxn. Most times, they don't even know it's there, until the conversation shifts to money and power. This row might challenge you, or maybe it won't. You never can tell until you dive in.

The Devil is the gatekeeper to the wild, and he will assist you in reclaiming the wild within your soul, the natural state of being for your spiritual self. This is not the "you" who tiptoes around social norms, trying to fit into a society that makes no logical sense. It is the wild you or the part of you that hears the messages in the wind, is deeply connected to the earth, and is guided by the goddess. This is your wild self, and the Devil wants you to reclaim it, own it, and walk proudly in your wild skin. It may seem ironic to be working with the Devil, considering you are fresh from the healing arms of the angel, Temperance. The astrological correspondence with the Devil is Capricorn, which means the Devil has staying power, doesn't know the meaning of giving up, and will stick with something until the job is done—now *that's* someone you want with you as you unlock the wild within. So perhaps Temperance knows well what she is doing when she sets you down at the Devil's door here at the beginning of the third row.

It is no surprise that the Tower comes next along the path of gateway three. In order to restore the wild parts of yourself, you will need to pull down everything that has kept it bound, tamed, and hidden. The Tower is the last part of your priestess initiation, and its energy and power force you to tear down the walls that you have built around yourself. You might consider this your priestess coming-out moment, where the world will finally get to see that which was held behind all of your walls. The Tower doesn't always have to be a dramatic experience; in fact, many people are happy to embrace its energy with ease and grace, letting it move through their daily experience, clearing obstacles from their path. No mess, no fuss. That all said, it really depends on how you have traveled through the first two gateways. If your journey was difficult, the Tower may make you feel exposed and vulnerable. If, however, your journey has been soul-guided, you are more than ready to have all the old come tumbling down around you. Either way, once the walls are nothing more than rubble, you will be left standing under the guiding light of the Star.

The Star is never too far away from the Moon. They travel together under the darkness of night, illuminating the sky. They are constant reminders that light will always find a way, even in the dark. Once all the rubble has settled and the Tower has moved past you, look to the sky. Let the Star guide you toward the growing light of the Moon. Allow the Star to be your beacon of hope in the crumbled mess of the past. The Star shows you that the journey has been worth it, that every step counted. It also gives you a map, a plan for what comes next as it directs you to the gravitational pull of the Moon.

In many respects, the Moon marks the end of your journey through the dark side of the soul; it is the card that allows you to howl, yell, and release all that darkness stored inside you. It is a phase which brings with it a deeper sense of the wild self, the self that cannot be bound, the self that only knows the primal energy of the earth. It is here, with the Moon's help, that you can finally slip out of your outdated costume, the one you have been wearing to fit in. Under the light of the Moon, give this armor back to the goddess and let yourself be naked, exposed, raw. Allow the Moon to bathe you, heal you, and reclaim you. Your time with the Moon is limited, because the Sun is coming. It is getting ready to rise; with it, your light will be restored.

Only in the darkness can we catch the spark of life, the fleck of light that bursts forth, wanting to catch and grow. The first rays of daylight slowly illuminate the tops of the trees, the peaks of the mountains, and the sky above. The Sun moves over the world in waves, taking time to reach the ground as it rises above the horizon line. With its rising so comes yours. The Sun card pulls back the final curtain on your dark journey and allows you to bring this newly claimed wild self into the light. The wild energies in which you have been initiated are not just for the dark moments in your life—they are for *all* of your life. As a priestess, you know how important it is to walk a wild line and feel that eternal connection to the earth, the universe, and yourself. The more the Sun illuminates your world, the more the wild settles into your bones, becoming one with you, your life, and your practice. In this respect you are reborn in the light. The Sun offers you a resurrection similar to the Death card, yet this time you have emerged from the underworld and find yourself very much back in the world.

This rebirth is only emphasized in the Judgement card, as yet another angel (this time Gabriel) sounds the trumpet to alert the world to your return. At the end of gateway three, you are a different person: you think differently and feel more deeply, your intuition has expanded, and your concept of self is both solid and malleable. As you embrace this version of yourself, you easily and effortlessly leave all thoughts of the past behind. You are happy for the blank slate that is now your life experience and walk confidently into the World.

In most journeys, we tend to end where we begin. The World card is both beginning and end. We've made a circular journey, though it can also be considered a spiral. The twenty-one cards of the major arcana repeat themselves inside the spiral, similar yet different each time we come back to them, always offering us the opportunity to walk the spiral in an expansive way or a contracted way, depending on which direction we face. For your journey, your feet face the potential of expansion. The World points you toward the next journey. It releases you at the end of gateway three and places you firmly on the path of the temples. This does not mean you cannot come back to the gateways—you will, often intentionally and habitually. The gateways represent the path of your life, which is why the Fool card is your Priestess card for your work here. As the priestess of your life, you will keep moving through the gateways again and again, always coming back to this point, the World.

The Devil and the Tower

"What is it you truly desire?" a voice whispers in your ear.

"Tell me," it continues, "what is your deepest darkest desire, the one that frightens you?" The Devil gives you a knowing smile as he leads you into the garden of liberation.

Here in the Devil's domain, you will need to learn to dance with the wild, untamed shadow part of yourself. You will need to become comfortable with desire; you need to know what you want, lest you become unable to create or manifest it in your life. In order to walk the priestess path, you need to first desire the journey. If you want to tap into the wisdom and guidance the goddess holds, you will need to be able to see your shadow reflected back to you and use your scars as points of learning. In order to find the truth in the light, you will first need to have understood the truth in the dark.

Do not be fooled—you are not meant to stay with your shadow for long. It is a point of healing and a place of liberation, not a permanent state of being. This is one of the biggest mistakes people make when doing shadow work. They linger too long and end up becoming stuck in the Devil's dominion. The point of looking at your shadow self is to see what you have placed there. What parts of you did you banish so you could fit in, be acceptable to others, and keep tame? Keeping these parts of yourself hidden has only caused you pain and suffering; now the Devil wants to help you free them and bring them into the light where they can be healed, transformed, and re-coded once and for all.

The Devil and the Tower work hand in hand here: once you have owned your desires, mastered your wants, and danced wildly with your shadow, life as you know it will fall at your feet.

All that once was will crumble, and the dust of your previous life will sift through your hands as it flows back into the sands of time. It is at this point of the priestess journey that you may decide that this is not for you. This part of the journey can break you, crack you open, and allow parts of you to be seen that you have spent your whole life hiding. The thought of being naked and exposed can be terrifying, but if you can stand among the wreckage of your life and own it, you will be free to search for the light, to seek the truth in what the light has to offer. The Devil and the Tower will have liberated you by guiding you through the dark.

Devotional Exercise

Before you take another step, define what "wild" means to you. One of the reasons I have not provided a definition is because the word means something different to everyone. I guess you could say that the wild devil in me is not the same as the wild devil in you. For this reason, everyone has a different experience with the Devil card. Rewilding yourself is part of the priestess path. You cannot walk it without spending time with the Devil and asking this card and archetype what it means to get in touch with your wild self. This step is therefore going to require you and the Devil to have a heart-to-heart.

Pull your Devil card from your deck. Light a candle, and spray an energy-clearing spray around your room. Pick up a pen and open a notebook. At the top of your page, write "My wild self is…" and start writing. Keep your Devil card in front of you as you write. Allow the energy and imagery of the card to prompt, poke, and nudge your discovery. Give yourself around ten minutes to write whatever comes to mind. Try not to edit or curate what you are writing or thinking. Allow it to flow unabridged as much as possible.

Once you have finished, take your Tower card and place it next to your Devil card. Use the spread that follows to see what changes stepping into this wild part of your priestess self will bring into your life. No matter how hard you try, you won't be able to keep things the same in your life once you step into the wild aspect of yourself. Even if your definition of wild isn't all that crazy, changes will happen. They seem small on the surface, but rest assured that they have the capacity to send deep and wide ripples into all areas of your life. This spread will help you better prepare for these changes and even give you a hint about what the goddess herself has in store for you now that you have allowed your wild self the space and opportunity to breathe. You will build this spread around your two central cards.

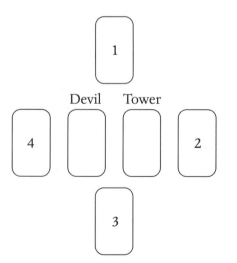

CARD ONE: What sort of changes will this bring into my career / professional life?

CARD TWO: What sort of changes will this bring into my relationships?

CARD THREE: What sort of changes will begin inside of myself?

CARD FOUR: What changes will the goddess demand?

Including the Devil and the Tower, you will have six cards before you: the Devil and the Tower in the middle and your four answers/guidance cards surrounding them. Go over this spread slowly. It's important to be kind and compassionate to yourself and any reactions you have to the cards that you have drawn. Remember that this energy will and does change. What you see today may very well be vastly different a month or two from now because you will either have become comfortable in this new wild energy or abandoned it altogether. There is no wrong or right way to deal with these cards and the energy they bring with them. Just take your time and breathe through it.

The Star, Moon, and Sun

It is interesting to note that after your Tower moment, once all the rubble and debris has settled and the dust has become one with the dirt, what you are left with is the Star. The guiding light of the goddess will be there to assist you, to remind you and shine for you. A priestess understands this breakdown-to-breakthrough event, this journey through the darkness back to the light. This is your moment to shine a light on the wild and untapped self, the self that has no limits and no bonds. Your Tower restriction lies broken and shattered at your feet. All the expectations of others are now nothing more than rubble. What is left is you—all of you, the dark and the light, the wild and socially constructed version of who you have been. Now that you've come to terms with what has been left behind after the Tower has had its way with you, the goddess wants you to think about what comes next. What happens now that there are no limits upon who and what you can be? What wishes do you send to the Star?

"Look to the sky, child of the earth, and tell me who you are" the goddess whispers in your ear. "When no one is looking, who do you become?"

This is the question your wild self needs to answer. The version of you that is always itching to come to the surface. The you that dances freely behind closed doors. Here in the shattered pieces of your carefully constructed identity you can bring that version of you into the light of the rising moon. Letting the moonbeams wash over you, cleansing you of the past and revealing the new you, the priestess version of yourself, the side of you connected to the wildness of your soul. As the moon shines on you like a giant spotlight, you feel this energy build in your body. You feel the sway in your hips, the tingling in your hands, the tapping of your feet. This need to move is growing and swelling, creating momentum like you have never known before. This is your wild energy, the energy of your divine self, complete and whole. This is how it feels to be fully embodied.

The more energized you become with this wild energy, your whole energy, the more light the moon gives. It is as if discovering the full aspects of yourself has allowed the moon to also grow in fullness. Wouldn't that be something, to know that your light, your energy, fills the moon? Maybe it does; the priestess understands her connection to the planets and stars through her devotion to the goddess. The beginning of light (albeit moonlight) lets you know that you are in the final phase of your pilgrimage. The journey begun at gateway one is drawing to an end. Although it is not over just yet, the emerging light and gathering energy of your soul lets you know that it is almost time for the sun to rise. In fact, if you turn now to the horizon you can see that there is a glow to it. Soon the sun and the moon will dance in the sky together and you will be illuminated yet again. You will be seen anew, different from when you first began, but not so different that you won't recognize yourself in the mirror.

As the glow on the horizon grows, tilt your head back and open your arms wide as if ready to embrace the coming light, opening yourself up to be blasted with the power and radiance that this new beginning has in store for you. You are, after all, facing east, the direction of newness. The new sun emerges into a new dawn, and you stand arms wide open with the new light of the day lapping at your toes. Waiting for it to fill you up and seal in all you have gained and heal all that you have lost. Breathe deeply now as you feel the warmth of the sun move up your legs, over your stomach, and upon your chest. You spread your arms even wider, allowing your heart to be fully exposed to the energy and power of the sun. The warmth continues up over your throat and onto your face. You keep your eyes closed for now, wanting to feel, not see; to sense instead of know. A few more breaths and you feel your whole body being bathed in the bright light of a new day. You can feel the difference in your energy from the tips of your toes to the top of your head. This must be how it feels to be reborn, to come from the darkness of the mother and into the light of the world of the senses, to go from comfort to having no place to hide. You open your eyes, ready to see this new self. Allow yourself to accept and recognize the new you that has been birthed through the act of pilgrimage. This is your moment. You blaze with rebellious renewal. You are illuminated from the inside out. You shine like the Star, Moon, and Sun. You are the goddess, and you have come home.

Devotional Exercise

It is not very often that we work with the energy of the Star, the Moon, and the Sun; generally speaking, we pick one of three. In this spread, we will be working with all three. This spread is a reminder of how light grows, and how each light has its own purpose and special magic. Remove the Star, Moon, and Sun cards from your deck before you begin the spread. Place them in the middle as in the image below:

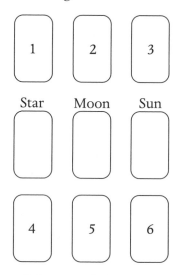

The top row of this spread shows conditions as they are right now. When you bring a situation, problem, or question to mind, just know that these cards are showing you here and now—the energy, emotion, lesson, or consequence of the "right now" experience. The bottom row shows you what is possible as you move from the light of the Star into the light of the Moon and then bring it all out into the open under the full glare of the Sun.

If you like, cleanse and/or clear the energy around your Star, Moon, and Sun cards before you begin. You could also light a candle, wave the smoke of an herb wand over your cards, and call the goddess in to assist you. This is not compulsory; it might, however, assist you in connecting more deeply to the information that the cards bring further for you. Once your space is set up, grab your deck (minus your Star, Moon, and Sun, of course) and give them a shuffle. Once you have finished shuffling, bring your question, problem, or inquiry to mind and see it form like a sentence on the screen of your mind. Then go ahead and draw your cards, placing them in the correct positions.

CARD ONE: What you can't change. The Star shines a light on what is left after the Tower card has had its way with you. What has not moved is what cannot be changed right now.

CARD TWO: What is hidden. It is easy not to see things in the dark, especially when the moon is in her darker phases. For now, there is enough light to show you what has been sitting in the shadows all this time.

CARD THREE: What you can change. Now that the Sun has influence, you will find things you can change.

CARD FOUR: What to take from the past. Now that you have taken a better look at the situation, it is time to make a plan to move forward. Here is what will benefit you.

CARD FIVE: Hopes and fears. Fear and excitement have the same charge—they share the same energy, and the body responds to them in similar ways. This card will show you what is about to spark your new journey.

CARD SIX: Positive influences. New adventure means a new mindset. It is time to train your mind to be positive leading and that starts by taking stock of the positive influences that surround you.

Once you have all of your cards drawn and you can see them, open your journal and begin taking notes. You may wish to pull out some of your favorite tarot books so you can study further. Just keep in mind that this spread is about the transformation you have undertaken along this last gateway of your Tarot Priestess journey. These cards are about you, your path, and who you are as you move through the invitations of the goddess. When you have finished your journal work, it would be a good idea to light a candle on your altar and give thanks to the goddess for all the changes she has offered you.* Use your Star, Moon, and Sun cards to craft a small prayer of thanks. Here's an example:

Dear Goddess: As I have come through the rubble of my past, I have claimed my wild self. The light of your star brought me back to the path. The moon watched over me as I traveled. Here I stand, arms wide open in the light of the sun with a grateful heart. Thank you, Goddess, for teaching me. Thank you, Goddess, for guiding me. Thank you, Goddess, for bringing me back to light. And so it is.

*Never leave a burning candle unattended.

Judgement and the World

You have come to the end of the third gateway. You have explored multiple ideas, learned many lessons, and now stand at the end of your journey. As with all journeys, you are not the same as you were when it began. For one thing, you have gotten deeper into your priestess path. You have started to see the world through the eyes of the goddess. Now it is time to decide if you will continue walking this path, moving on to the next phase of your journey and exploring the four temples. The first step is to claim this new identity, allowing yourself to be seen anew, free from the past and all things that bind you to the old self. Judgement asks you to walk cleanly, dripping no residue of the you who started this journey. You have been healed, cleansed, and made anew. But only you can decide whether this is who you wish to be and continue to become. The great thing about identities is that we can create them, reject them, rebuild them, and then accept them.

Will you accept the new identity? It seems like a simple question, but Judgement knows the many threads that bind human memory to the past. Ask her and she will cut them, releasing you from all that has come before. Starting fresh isn't easy, but it is simple. Just don't look back. Don't turn your head. Resist the urge to peer over your shoulder. And most importantly, do not go digging around in the graves of things that you released and let go of along your journey to this moment. Judgement asks you instead to look forward. Keep your head up and shoulders back. Open your heart and allow new experiences to unfold. Meet the World as this new self. For the new you has different beliefs, is seeking more soul-aligned opportunities, and is taking action based on nudges and prompts from the goddess. This priestess identity you are slipping on is devotional.

It is about going deeper, not wider. You will now see the World not as a place but as part of who you are. Judgement asks you to see what is outside of you not as separate from yourself, but instead as extension of the new you.

So who is the new you? The World may mark the end of your journey through the three gateways, but it also reminds you that all journeys end where they begin: at home. In this way, the World is your homecoming, to the self, and to the version of you that has always been there but was not as embodied and expressed as it is now. And really, coming home to the self is all this journey has been about—to make you feel confident, calm, and powerful in your own skin. See all of yourself and accept it with radical self-love. See yourself as the goddess sees you— perfectly imperfect, whole yet broken, and uniquely you. The divine aspect of who you are is not about the costume or being accepted by others; it isn't even about the accolades. It is about knowing you are worthy because you exist. You never need a why, you just needed to be. And the World opens its arms to you as a reminder of this.

Yet even though you are back where you started, things around you will feel different. Perhaps they even look different. Your perception has shifted. Your awareness of yourself and the world around you is not the same as it was before you started your journey through the gateways. How you move through the world will also have changed. So do not worry if you feel different about where you now stand—this is normal. You may need to reorganize your world a little to make it more aligned to the energy you now embody. You may even need to change how you look, dress, and present yourself. For some, these external changes will be minor. For others, the need to see the outer self express the new inner self may be more extreme. Only you will know how you wish to be in the world now. Just remember you still have the temples to work through. Your journey isn't over. In fact, you will come back to this point over and over again, making minor adjustments to your life as you return, over and over again. The World knows where you begin and end—and where you end is where you begin.

Devotional Exercise

Landing on this page means you have made it through the first three gateways of your priestess path. You have walked with, played with, and learned from the archetypes of the major arcana. You have walked the spiral and come back to where you started, but this is not the same place. It might look similar, but it will feel different. *You* most definitely will be different than when you began. We need only have one new thought, clear one old belief, adjust our energy, or release one small block in order to be a new vibrational person. The tiniest of adjustments to our overall being create a new version of ourselves. And as you come to the end of this gateway, you have had one small change happen inside of you. It might be so deep that you may not have noticed it with your conscious mind yet, but you will see it show up in the near future. The goddess will send you a sign, a knowing that you will not be able to ignore. You will see, even if you don't yet believe.

To wrap both this chapter and the conclusion of the gateways up, let's do a little clean-up work before you step out into the World and head towards the temples. Remove your Judgement card from your deck and place it on your altar. If you do not have an altar, simply place it faceup in front of you. If you have some clear quartz crystal or selenite, grab that as well, to place in your left hand. If you don't have any crystals, imagine you are holding a beautiful crystal in your left hand. Keep your eyes focused on your Judgement card and take a deep, slow breath in through the nose and out through the mouth. Repeat this deep slow breath three more times, relaxing both your body and your mind. Allow your shoulders to drop, relaxing the body with each breath.

Now, close your eyes and imagine the energy from your crystal starting to grow and move out of your hand to the top of your head. Watch as this energy starts to shower down on you, washing you. Starting at the top of your head, it moves down your arms, over your face, through your chest. Just keep watching as this crystal energy cleanses you, and say the following mantra: "I release you. I reset you." This mantra allows you to be reborn in many respects, to set yourself free from the past under the loving and protective gaze of Judgement. When the crystal energy stops flowing, which it will, stop the mantra. Take another set of three deep breaths and gently open your eyes. Roll your neck and stretch your arms and legs to get the energy flowing through them. Thank your crystal—physical or imagined—and put it back.

Pick up your deck of tarot cards and give them a shuffle. Now ask the World: "What gifts does this ending bring me?" Flip a card and see what the World has told you. You can take this card and the World card to your journal if you wish to explore it further.

We are now done with our journey through the gateways. In the next part, we will move on to the different stages of Tarot Priestess. As we move through these stages and points of initiation, you will be working exclusively with your court cards. You might want to remove them now and prepare for your next adventure.

PART TWO

Walking the priestess path isn't about the costume, nor is it about doing things the same way as someone else. It is about finding your own personal way to embody the devotional path of the goddess. One of the things that can be a real struggle to those coming to the priestess path—that I know was true for me—is that I had a very biased idea of what a priestess looked like, sounded like, and acted like. None of these ideas were true, but it took me time to bust the myth I had created in my head. I also realized that this sort of embedded bias about devotional work is pretty widespread across all spiritual practices. Society has done a pretty good job brainwashing all of us when it comes to what is considered spiritual and what is dismissed as fake, evil, or even a scam. Unfortunately, most of what is lumped into the latter is deeply rooted within feminine spiritual practices and, by default, the work of a living priestess. Having a connection to the divine goddess, living an intuitive and inspired life, working with nature, and wanting to heal one's community are not fake or a con; it is very much a valid devotional path.

In part two, you are going to find sixteen very different ways to show up, embody, and slip into the role of priestess. You may find one that fits you instantly or maybe you still need more time to feel into the options. We will be exploring these sixteen different priestess styles with the tarot court cards; as these are the people of the deck, these cards lend themselves beautifully for embodying work. To be very clear on what I mean when I use the word "embody" here, I mean finding one role that sounds and feels like you, one that resonates with how you deal with devotional work and how you see yourself as a spiritual traveler. (At the very least, it's how you see yourself right now.) When you find your court card self, you will use it as a guide to assist you in embodying your priestess self, as a way to see yourself as the priestess you are and have always been, even if it's at the Page stage. Some will move through the court cards daily, weekly, or even monthly as we continue to deepen our connection to the goddess and make our Tarot Priestess work a more regular practice. Wherever you are and however you wish to show up is perfect!

There is a very specific way part two works with what follows after it. The court cards here work with the temples. Because the court cards themselves are a part of the four tarot suits of the minor arcana, once you have selected your priestess style or card that feels and sounds like you, you'll want to see what temple it belongs to. From there, you can then do one of two things. The first is bibliomancy—flip to the chapter that corresponds to that temple and randomly stop on a page somewhere to find out what that temple goddess wants you to know for the day. This will give you another card to work with alongside your court card. Alternatively, you can divide your tarot deck up into suits, aces to tens, pick up the corresponding suit, give it a shuffle, and select a card. Now you will have two cards laid out in front of you to read.

Want to take this process a step further? Select a major arcana card and see what gateway this message is connected with. Again, you can do it the bibliomancy way by going to a page in part one, or you can select a major arcana card from your deck by shuffling your twenty-one (minus the Fool) major cards and drawing one, resulting in a three-card spread. You can use these cards to journal with, give you a daily message from the goddess, or even set your altar for the day. This is a lovely way to see how you are showing up as your priestess self, and what blessings you are receiving or what healing work still needs to be done. As a note on the temples, once you have gotten more comfortable with working with the cards this way, you can start selecting your temple card from any of the temples. Just give yourself permission to take time and get comfortable with working with the goddess in this new way first.

You are now fully prepped and ready to dive into the next chapter. Move at your own pace through the court card section and see which one feels, sounds, and attunes to who you are now and who you see yourself becoming along this new journey of Tarot Priestess. Each card is special, none is better than another; they are just different experiences. May the goddess guide you.

Chapter Four

THE FOUR STEPS
OF INITIATION

From Pages to Kings

───────────)) ● ((───────────

In this chapter, you are going to explore the four main initiation stages of the priestess path. We will be using the tarot court cards to assist in identifying and working with each level of these positions. These positions align to the areas of the temple you could work, study, or engage in during your temple time. Just know that it doesn't matter where you are or where you want to be. All that is required here in this step is for you to get an understanding of the levels, what they do, and how they play a part in the bigger temple and priestess process. All spiritual journeys have an initiation process, and there is one built right into the major arcana of the tarot, known as the Fool's journey. Earlier, I shared what the Fool represents and how it will be used, so from here think of the court cards as how the Fool would embody themselves along the initiation path. The Fool starts as a Neophyte, moves into the second row of the major arcana as the Acolyte, enters priestess training in the third row, and brings it all together as a High Priestess at the completion of the World card. You can follow this journey through the four temples (or suits) of the tarot as well; here we are using the court cards for the journey taken with the Fool.

Each stage does something different to you. They put you in a different mindset and change your energetic vibration, and they do so without any real conscious awareness on your part. That's the lovely part of a journey—change and transformation tend to sneak up on you after the fact. In much the same way, you will travel through the temples and embody each of the four stages of initiation. This chapter is a guide and reference point for the remainder of your adventure with the goddess and the priestess path. Each court card will have its own lesson, values, and standards for daily practice. Everything required for each level is spelled out for you, so all you have to do is follow the court cards; let them take the lead.

Neophyte/Page

To the novice, the beginner, the one who is just starting on the path of priestess studies: welcome. At this level, you are very much walking in the Page's shoes. You have come across this topic and are only now starting to learn. You are gathering as much information as possible before you decide whether you wish to proceed to the next level or not. Here in the realm of the Neophyte, you have yet to decide which temple you wish to study in, so all of them are open to exploration. Luckily for you, there are four temples for you to poke around in. Just remember that a Page is seen and not heard. Whatever you read may very well serve as your Neophyte initiation, as this may be the first time you have ever explored the priestess path. If that is the case, the goddesses and I welcome you. Please come in and make yourself comfortable. Make sure to write a nice list of respectful questions and wait patiently as they are answered. Like the good Page you are, you may also want to make sure you have notebooks, pens, and snacks with you at all times. You never know which temple may entice you, so you want to make sure you are prepared to stay a while if something peaks your curiosity or sparks your inner priestess.

Daily Practice with the Pages

The following exercise can be done for as long as you feel the need to connect with the energy of the Neophyte. This is your beginning phase with the goddess, and you can spend as much time here as you wish. You may also wish to do this at your altar or in your meditation space.

To begin, remove the four Pages from your deck. Place them facedown and give them a little shuffle. Collect them, keeping them facedown, and hold them to your heart. Close your eyes, take a few deep breaths, and connect to the energy of the goddess. Ask the goddess to flow through you and show you which temple she would like you to work with today. When you feel ready, place the cards facing down in front of you. Spread them out and choose just one card. This is your Page for today, the lesson the goddess has requested you sit with and the temple with whose energy she wishes to surround you. You can now journal with, meditate on, or even draw one card from the rest of your deck to see what action step would best serve you to deeper connect with the lesson and energy for your day. The manner in which you move through this lesson is entirely up to you.

Neophyte of Danu: Page of Pentacles

To walk this temple, you will first need to remove your shoes as the soles of your feet will need to be in constant contact with the earth. You must feel the energy of the goddess as she tickles your toes and connects you to the world of physicality. In this temple, you need to be willing to get your hands dirty—just like your feet, you may often find them in the dirt. You will learn that all that you need is already given, that you were born from the abundance of natural supply and cannot ask for anything that the goddess has not already created with her own two hands. The Page of Pentacles is a steady student who takes their time and is not in a hurry to move forward. This is just as well; there's much to learn in the present moment. The ground where you stand has an abundance of lessons to teach and many a secret to tell, so have your notebook at the ready because you just never know when the gift of the goddess will be handed to you.

Neophyte of Saraswati: Page of Swords

This temple is not at all like the one of dirt and mud. The lessons here are sharp and can oftentimes be painful. You must be on alert if you do not wish to cut yourself. That said, the goddess is not cruel—she wants only your greatest joy and happiness at all times. However, she also knows that in order for you to receive the gift of peace, love, and divine understanding from her, you must first learn what a gift your mind truly is. The first initiation into the Temple of Swords is to understand that your mind is not a burden; it does not exist to cause you suffering or make your life difficult. The mind is a gift of unlimited and untapped potential. In the right hands and with the right amount of training, the Page of Swords can conquer fear itself.

Just make sure you have a packet of bandages in your backpack, because I guarantee that you are going to get the odd cut here and there. Some cuts will be deeper than others, but none will be wounds you cannot heal.

Neophyte of Lilith: Page of Wands

The Temple of Wands will tease you, taunt you, and possibly even burn you. Sometimes you will find yourself in the dark, while other times you will be surrounded by fire. Before that, however, you have to learn how to create a spark—you can't have a fire without having one first. The goddess knows all about sparks, flames, fires, and what is needed to light up, stay lit, and how to feed that fire. She is willing to teach you all that she knows, though I suggest making sure that your clothes aren't highly flammable, notebooks aren't made of paper, and that your hair is tied safely away from your face. Fire is unpredictable, so you must learn how to predict its energy to the best of your ability. The Page of Wands isn't the type of student who does well in a traditional classroom setting. This Page likes their lesson in a more explosive environment. Thankfully, the goddess keeps a lake nearby just in case. So grab your burn cream, a few bandages, and maybe stuff a fire extinguisher in your backpack—the temple of Lilith is ready for you now.

Neophyte of Avalon: Page of Cups

From the lake she appears, cup in hand and arm outstretched. She offers you the chalice and wants to know if you are ready to take a sip. She sees your scars and wants to heal you. She wants to show you how to use your emotions as powerful tools for success, love, and abundance, but first you have to dip your fingers into the cup. This is your first initiation into the priesthood of Avalon. The goddess of the lake shows you how to take the water from your fingertips and anoint yourself: first at the heart, then at the third eye, then to the crown, then to the navel, and finishing with the throat. This simple act of touching your body connects you to that which you are made from: water. That water flows through you, tiny rivers of life just like the ones that run through the world outside you. This similarity is not a coincidence—the world outside you mirrors the world within you. The Temple of Cups has much to teach you about this mirror world, about the emotions that create it. The Page of Cups paints with a sensitive palette and is often shocked at the world they have created. Sometimes that world is of the Page's great and fantastical dreams, and other times it is one of nightmares. But here in this Temple of Cups with the Priestesses of Avalon, you will learn how to use this sensitivity to create unparalleled beauty. So dip your fingers in the cup and let the lessons begin.

Acolyte/Knight

Discipline, ritual, and habitual tasks are the life of the Acolyte. An essential part of the temple, Acolytes keep all of the day-to-day aspects of temple life in order. From lighting candles, to cleaning, to making sure the new initiates are taken care of, these knights of the temple are always on call and ready to serve. In fact, the knights are the very first people you see in the temple: they will greet you with a smile and ask you to join them as they make their rounds. They will show you all the important parts of the temple grounds and answer any questions you have about the goddess. This is the next level along the priestess path. You have decided that after gathering your information, you want to know more. You want to get to know the ways of the goddess and the temple in a more practical way. Acolyte is a hands-on position, and depending on which temple you are assigned to, you may even have to travel. Your initiation at this level will also be a practical one. You will make your vow to the goddess and agree to temple life and everything it involves. Perhaps you arrived as an Acolyte and this is just one more piece of your practice or one more tool to help you stay on your chosen path. If so, keep reading. Continue through the work and decide if you will forever stay at this level or if you are working your way into the role of priestess.

Daily Practice with the Knights

This exercise can be done for as long as you feel the need to connect with the energy of the Acolyte. Here, you will see what sort of training the goddess has in store for you today. Remember that at this level, you learn about habits, techniques, and daily practice. You may wish to do this exercise at your altar or in your meditation space. To begin, remove the four knights from your deck, place them facedown, and give them a little shuffle. Collect them up, keeping the face of the cards where you cannot see them, and place these four cards at your navel point. Close your eyes, take a few deep breaths, and connect to the energy of the goddess. Ask the goddess to flow through you and show you which temple she would like you to work with today. When you feel ready, place the cards back down in front of you, keeping them facedown, spread them out, and choose just one card. This is your knight for today; this is the temple she wishes you to train with and the new skills she wishes for you to learn. You can now journal with this card, meditate with this card, or even draw one card from the rest of your deck to see how this card will assist you in your training.

Acolyte of Danu: Knight of Pentacles

At this level of initiation you have dedicated yourself to the temple's mundane tasks. It is your job to check supplies and ensure things are where they are meant to be for ritual and ceremony. As the Knight of Pentacles, you will be keeping detailed accounts of all comings and goings to the temple and recording all the daily activities of the temple itself. The more detailed your records, the happier you will be. As an Acolyte of Danu, this will be in daily practice. Your day will have structure, purpose, and meaning to it. Every task you do will be a devotional act to the goddess herself, and your discipline and commitment to your practice will become a living prayer. In this temple, you know that your day will move at a much slower pace than what others are accustomed to. There is no rushing and hustling here in this temple of earth; in this place, things take time and have their own cycles. As an Acolyte of Danu, your days are spent learning to slow down, to get into the natural rhythms of the day, and to act in a focused and methodical way, one that requires patience and skill.

Acolyte of Saraswati: Knight of Swords

There is much to be done: records to keep, prayers to write, and meditations to sit with. Here in the temple of the air goddess, you will learn to use your mind as both a weapon of knowledge and peace. You will start your day in meditation, beginning in the dark and finishing in the light, a reminder that we come to our practice seeking the light of awakening from the darkness of suffering. Shifting from suffering to awakening requires enough discipline to wait until the darkness recedes before committing to the coming day. Once the Acolyte of Saraswati has left the meditation mat, it is time to write the goddess's teachings, putting into words the messages and instruction she has for her students. Knowledge is power; those who understand this wield the most powerful weapon in existence. But it takes time, practice, and discipline to use this sword. One must understand that the blade of this temple is double-edged—and both are sharp. It is the knight's job to train with this sword day in and day out to become stronger in body and mind; sharper and more deliberate; and to attain new levels of understanding, compassion, and forgiveness. The Acolyte of Saraswati is committed to releasing themselves and others from suffering. Their weapon of liberation is the mind.

Acolyte of Lilith: Knight of Wands

Not all Acolytes are destined to sit in quiet stillness. Here in the temple of fire, the devotional act is not stillness. The Acolyte of Lilith will not be found in quiet reverence. In this place, movement is the way to the goddess. The devotional tool is sacred dance. Here the energy of the Knight of Wands can come out and move, shake, and form in sacred union with the goddess. The Acolyte of the temple of fire knows how to bring the heat to any ceremony or ritual as sacred desire swirls inside them, flowing out into the space they inhabit through movement. Energy, power, and passion are stomped into the earth at the meeting of these acolytes, their soles dancing over the grass and dirt of the temple courtyard. This form of connection to divine energy allows this Knight of fire to radiate—to illuminate the path to all those who come seeking the knowledge and wisdom of the goddess. As an Acolyte of Lilith, you understand that you need to embody the light in order to share the light.

Acolyte of Avalon: Knight of Cups
If gazing into a chalice filled with water hoping to catch glimpses of the future is not your idea of a good time, then this initiation may not be for you. The Acolyte of Avalon must train in the art of water scrying. They must be able to gaze into the stillness and see beyond one's reflection. This level of training is not for the faint-hearted or those who cannot sit still. The act of quiet stillness is all in a day's work for this dreamy yet insightful Knight. It is within this Knight's nature to look for signs, flashes of inspiration, and dreams inside the water. In this initiation, one's intuition is awakened. The second sight is a prized gift and one most commit to all that comes with understanding it. This temple is where one comes when they wish to be instructed in the art of depth and flow—where you must shift your perception and look beyond what you think you see. This temple will teach you to master your emotions so you can see clearly. The Acolyte of Avalon is not an easy position to hold. The initiation is long, the healing is intense, and the commitment is ongoing. You must learn not only how to deal with the reflection of the world around you but also how your projection on it alters the very reality you experience. The High Priestess of Avalon teaches you that cup gazing is more potent and powerful than you could possibly ever imagine.

Priestess/Queen
You have moved up from Acolyte to Priestess. You have taken your next lot of vows to not only serve the goddess but also her

followers. You have moved into the next phase of devotion and service. At this level of temple life your day is now about how you can perform tasks and rituals that benefit the larger community. People will now come to you with their problems and concerns and expect you to assist them. You will not turn them away, but instead navigate them through the teachings of the goddess and the many lessons of the temple that are relevant to their needs or concerns. You may also find yourself having a much larger role to play in organizing fundraising events and connecting people. You now walk with new robes and everywhere you go people know who you are. They seek you out and have a level of expectation of your presence. This is why the life of priestess is not for everyone. But you have made it this far. You have decided to devote your life to the goddess and be her servant here in the physical realm. It will be at this level of service that you will notice all areas of your life upgraded as well. You will have more energy, more time, more health, more mental clarity, and more joy than you ever thought possible. So are the gifts of service.

Daily Practice with the Queens

At the level of Queen, you may add this exercise to your daily or weekly practice; this is part of your devotional work as a priestess. It is at this level your daily practice will deepen and become more about your inner divinity and the strengthening of your bond to the goddess. You may wish to do this exercise at your altar or in your meditation space. To begin, remove the four Queens from your deck, place them facedown, and give them a little shuffle. Collect them while keeping them facedown, and hold them to your heart center. Close your eyes, take a few deep breaths, and connect to the energy of the goddess. Ask the goddess to flow through you and show you which temple she wants you to deepen your connection to today. When you feel ready, place the cards back down in front of you, keeping them facedown, spread them out, and choose just one card. This is your Queen for today and the temple she wishes you to go deeper with. This card represents how the goddess wishes to connect with you. You can now journal with this card, meditate with this card, or even draw one card from the rest of your deck to see what step you can take today to strengthen your practice.

Priestess of Danu: Queen of Pentacles

As a priestess of the temple of Danu, your days will be filled with service to both goddess and local community. Your mornings will start in prayer, connecting your energy to the goddess and opening yourself up to be a vessel for her earth-based lessons. The Queen of Pentacles knows that connection is key to abundance. Connection to Danu's energy brings an abundance of healing energy as well as physical resources. The two allow you to move into your community and teach just how the goddess provides because your life is the lesson of the goddess: You live through divine supply and thus teach about divine supply. Your connection to the goddess means you know the goddess's supply is unlimited. Through interaction with your community, you establish other links and connections, ones that help you with your mission and allow you to continue being of service to the temple and the goddess. These community connections could come in the form of donations and benefactors. It is the Queen's pleasure to deal with this form of devotional practice. Running the temple coffers will be one of your responsibilities as priestess, and you will do it with grace, reverence, and ceremony.

Priestess of Saraswati: Queen of Swords

As a priestess of this temple, you will start your day with a deep mindfulness practice. You understand that being able to dictate the terms of the ego mind is the best way to honor the goddess. Once the ego mind is under control, you can open your direct connection to the goddess and allow divine consciousness into your day. This direct connection to goddess consciousness is the gift you bring to your larger community. Through it, you can teach your community how to meditate, shift their beliefs, and how to bring their thoughts into alignment with the vortex of blessings the goddess has created for them. By working with the energy of swords, you can bring lack-based and scarcity mindsets to an end, moving yourself and all those around you into a state of abundant health, joy, wealth, and happiness. You know as the priestess of this temple that everything starts in one's head and that the end of all suffering can be gained collectively—it's just a matter of training those around you to master their own minds.

Priestess of Lilith: Queen of Wands

Here in the Temple of Wands, you are the priestess of fire. You have moved from learning how to spark the Divine in yourself to now showing others how to do the same. Your lessons are in light, energy, and radiance. Showing your community how to shine and be a beacon of strength, hope, and unity is what you have trained so long to do. The goddess Lilith does not tolerate excuses; she gets things done. She wants results and she knows that the light brings these results and as her humble servant, you too will be the bringer of results. All those around you will feel your intensity and power; like the Queen of Wands, you will bring light to the darkness, warm the hearts of those who have felt alone, and spark desire in those who have lost faith. Your role as priestess in this temple will be action-packed. Beginning your mornings with yoga, your body will flow and burn through cycles, and your physical vessel will be an instrument of the light. Never again will you doubt your ability to serve yourself and your community.

Priestess of Avalon: Queen of Cups
The priestess of Avalon brings love to all those who seek it. She is a cheerleader and champion of all those who have an open heart. She does not judge whether the heart is whole or has been broken into pieces—all she cares about is if it is open and willing to try again. Emotions run deep in this temple, so it is necessary to know how to navigate them. Your training at this level of initiation will be one of counselor, healer, and motivator. The Queen of Cups is overflowing with grace, empathy, and compassion. She knows that those in her community who grace the temple's steps with earnestness need her assistance. She does not turn others away but instead makes more space in her heart for them. This priestess is a true heart-centered leader. Your days as a priestess of Avalon will begin with a water ritual—perhaps the making of tea, or blessing the many water bowls around the temple itself. Water is a life-giving gift and it is to be honored and celebrated each and every day.

High Priestess/King

If you have decided to receive this level of initiation, then you know in your core you came into this incarnation to give yourself to something much larger than you and your earthly experience. You also made agreements of responsibility, discipline, and commitment to the goddess. The High Priestess is the ruler of the entire temple—the rule, the law, and the divine vessel, opened to the goddess to work through her. At this level, you have made the temple a holy kingdom, a space of sacred life where all your devotees are protected, nourished, and safe. You have agreed to build, maintain, and run a sanctuary for those who seek the goddess. You will be Mother, Father, Teacher, and humble servant. You will rule on high and pray on your knees. You will be the direct link to the goddess, her teachings, and wisdom on the earthly plane. In your temple, the work of the goddess will be done.

Daily Practice with the Kings

At the top level of the priestess initiation ladder, it is your job to think about how you will lead your temple, manage your followers, and strengthen the bonds between the goddess and the larger community. Your daily practice is different from all the previous levels because you have to balance personal spiritual development with the spiritual development of those under you, which means that every lesson, message, sign, and ritual will have a dual aspect to it. This balance requires all the skills you have learned from the Page, Knight, and Queen levels. Here you will bring it all together in this daily practice. You may wish to do this exercise at your altar or in your meditation space. To begin, remove the four Kings from your deck. Place them facedown and shuffle them. Next, collect them, keeping them facedown, and hold these four cards at your navel point. Close your eyes, take a few deep breaths, and connect to the energy of the goddess. Ask the goddess to hold you steady, clear your mind, and make you an instrument of her work. When you feel ready, place the cards in front of you, keeping them facedown. Spread them out and choose just one card. This is your King for today and the temple the goddess wishes you to grow and nurture today. This card is the energy you will lead with and assist others with as you move through the next twenty-four hours. You can journal with this card or meditate with it, or even draw another single card from the rest of your deck to see what step you can take to use this energy not just for yourself but for those who come to you seeking guidance and reassurance.

High Priestess of Danu: King of Pentacles

The High Priestess of the Temple of Pentacles has money on her mind; all the priestesses under her charge live in a world that requires money and other material things. These material things often end up in the hands of those who come to the temple seeking help. In order to ensure all are taken care of, the High Priestess must make sure there is always more coming in than there is going out. This King loves dealing with numbers, engaging in deals, and gets tremendous pleasure in being able to provide for all their kingdom. In this case, the temple is the kingdom. There is a level of mastery here in the realm of resources that is impressive and often something others strive to replicate. Yet the High Priestess of Danu knows that to get to this level requires disciplined steps. You have to train your mind to see opportunities others do not. You have to constantly move through your excuses and never let yourself get comfortable. Expansion is easy when you understand it isn't simple. When you step up to this level of initiation, you understand the burden you are about to carry and do it with a smile on your face. You know you are ready, able, and capable of keeping your temple thriving. You understand your main point of service is to keep the revenue rolling in.

High Priestess of Saraswati: King of Swords

Here in the Temple of Swords, the High Priestess is decisive, firm, and deliberate. There is no room for doubt at this level of initiation. You have to trust that your decisions are the right ones and leave all fears at the door. There is no space for procrastination in this temple—it could cost the temple and its other priestesses dearly. For this reason, the King of Swords isn't in a rush to make up their mind. They prefer to have all the facts laid out before them and understand the full consequences of the direction a decision will create. This amount of information-gathering takes the fear out of the process and allows them to get comfortable with consequences. The High Priestess also understands that decision-making is an art form, one learned over time with hours of practice. The High Priestess also knows that being a good steward of one's mind, thoughts, and beliefs means not asking whether the right decision is being made; instead, there is firm belief that whatever decision is made will be the right one. There is nuance in this mindset that only years of mental training can create.

High Priestess of Lilith: King of Wands

There is beauty in movement—a catch of the breath, a glint in the eye, and quickening of the pulse. The rush of accomplishment and the thrill of success wrap this High Priestess in a blanket of burning desire. This High Priestess moves through the day with purpose, expectancy, and passion. Everything at this level of initiation has an edge to it, a rush, something that makes you feel alive and on fire with divine energy. Right here in the temple of Lilith is where the ecstatic nature of your spiritual journey will come to a head. The King of Wands likes to see things catch fire, be it a thought, feeling, or a desire. The heat and intensity of this fire is what drives the energy of this temple. The quest is for something more, but not on a material level— no, here the quest is deeper. Lilith is not overly impressed with the trinkets of the outside world; she is more interested in finding your light, brightening your spark, and making you glow for the whole world to see. The High Priestess of the Temple of Wands follows in her goddess's footsteps, showing up in the community to find the light in all those who seek her spiritual guidance.

High Priestess of Avalon: King of Cups

The High Priestess of Avalon is in the business of legend creation. She is the ultimate empath and uses this skill to empower others so that they can step up and fulfill their divine destiny. The High Priestess does not see her feelings or sensitivities as weaknesses; instead, she sees them as a superpower. That superpower has shaped her, refined her skill and expertise, and made her who she is today. You cannot get to this level of initiation without having earned a few emotional scars along the way, and it is through those very scars that this King identifies greatness in others. There is skill to seeing those who are destined to be more than they believe they can be. There is an art to holding space for others to find their own light so they can shine. The High Priestess of Avalon knows how to do this; they have trained for the sacred act of ascension—not of the self but of those whom they serve.

★ ★ ★

The path to the goddess is many and varied. Throughout this chapter you have explored sixteen different ways you can work, learn, and move along that path. As you progress from here, you will also notice that you will find yourself at different stages of the initiation process. Each temple will offer you a chance to explore one or all four of its levels. You can decide how long you choose to stay at each stage. For example, you may find you spend more time at the Page level in one temple and the Queen level in another. Any amount of time is fine—we all have different ways of coming before the goddess to seek her counsel. Sometimes we are the novice, hearing the teachings of the cards for the very first time, and at other times we are High Priestess, sharing stories of the arcana with all who seek a more spiritually aligned life. Only you will know which stage you are at when you come before the temple steps. The goddess will always accept you where you are and will continue to work to get you where you want to be.

Part Three: The Temples

Welcome to part three of your journey. In this part, you will begin your journey through the four temples, also known as the tarot suits. Each temple corresponds to a suit in the minor arcana and is dedicated to a goddess who has provided lessons through the cards, ace to ten. These lessons, journeys, and devotional exercises are all part of your Tarot Priestess training, covering your mind, emotions, inner light, and connection with the material and your body. The goddesses you will meet here are not the only ones you can work with along the way, but they are ones you will walk with in order to learn what is needed here. They are the ones who presented themselves to instructors for this Tarot Priestess journey.

You are about to experience the aces through tens in a totally different way than you ever have before. Maybe you will like this new way of working with the minor arcana or perhaps this temple work is just not for you moving forward. All I ask is that you at least stick with it for the duration of the book and do as many devotional exercises as you can. The more you engage with the temples, the more the goddess and the cards can assist you. The best way to work with this part is to divide your tarot cards into suits and then in order: ace, two, three, four, five, six, seven, eight, nine, ten. Keep the suit or temple you are working with near you at all times as you work through the exercises. I would also recommend having a second deck ready to assist with spreads.

If you are new to goddess work, let these chapters serve as your introduction. Do your best to let each of the goddesses into your mind, heart, and energy. You may even notice them appearing in real life as you make your way through the temples. For example, you might get an email about something named Avalon or meet someone named Lilith. Perhaps someone at your job knows all about Saraswati, and you might even stumble into a book at the library about Danu. The work in the temples may bring other goddesses to you, so be on the lookout—the goddess wears many faces and is happy to show up in a way that is most appealing to you. I also highly recommend setting up an altar to each of the temple goddesses as you work with them (altar spaces are covered in part one).

Your goddess altar will anchor your work with the goddess and get you into the habit of doing daily tarot rituals. Setting up your altar each morning will be part of your Tarot Priestess work, which for some will become a lifelong habit, just as it is now mine. I can't even imagine my life without my Tarot Priestess altar; it holds space for healing, prayer, abundance, support, guidance, and expansion. When I need to focus, I set up my altar, light my candle, and call for the goddess. She steadies my mind, calms the beat of my heart, and whispers words of encouragement in my ears. I called her many times while writing this book and set up many an altar to hold the energy of productivity and momentum. I meditated, prayed, gave offerings, and chanted at my altar, asking the goddess to use me as her vessel, clear my blocks, and ease my doubts.

What follows are simple practices with powerful results. It is now your turn to sit before the temple goddesses to honor them, listen to them, and open yourself to them. So grab your cards, set up your altar, and begin your journey into the temples.

Chapter Five

The Temple of Pentacles

**Connecting to Earthly Devotion:
Priestessing with the Daughters of Danu**

)) ● ((

Ode to Danu

She bends at the knee

Hem dipping into the water

Scooping mud from the riverbank

Throwing it into a woven basket

Water drips from the bottom

Slowly separating the solids

What will not be used goes back to the river

For nothing is ever wasted

She keeps collecting until she is satisfied

Letting the basket continue to drain

Hanging it from a hook in a nearby tree

The goddess prepares for her creation

Child of dirt

Child of earth

She checks the basket pressing lightly into the mud

Making sure the water keeps seeping away

Flowing back to whence it came

A click and a smirk is all it takes

For this mud is ready to create

On the table of fallen tree

She kneads and molds with the greatest of ease

The goddess sings, she swirls and plays

While putting the life into the river clay

The child of dirt

The child of earth

Slowly starts to take its shape

Head, hands, feet

The outer being all but done

Yet something is missing

This child is undone

Heart and soul is what it needs

To care for the mother in the souls of its feet

From out her pocket she pulls a star

Places it gentle into its chest

Breathing in deep she begins to blow

Watching as the child of dirt now glows

Light emanates from the star seed inside

Radiating

Bright

Auric and true

The goddess places the child upon its feet

Slowly it comes to life

Eyes wide open

Hands held tight

"Come to me, child," the goddess commands

"I am your mother and I bring you gifts."

The child moves unsure

On unstable feet

Wobbling and waving with each star beat

"Hold out your hand" the mother instructs

The child of earth releases its fist

An outstretched hand is now on offer

The goddess smiles and clucks once more

Then from her pocket she pulls a coin

Gold and sparkly

Catching in the sun

The child watches carefully as the coins makes contact with her new skin

Flesh made of mud and sand

She turns it over and raises her eyes

Questioning beams from her to the coin

"It is your reminder"

The goddess replies

"That you shall want for nothing in this land of my
making. Ask and it is yours no matter the request.
So remember, mud child, to only ask for the best.
This world that is yours only wants to give. So
watch your heart and mind your lips."

The child looks down and squeals in delight

Running from the mother in her fancy flight

The goddess sighs and bends once more

Child one million, to one million more

Back to scooping the mother now bends

The land is plenty

The task never ends.

Introduction to the Temple of Pentacles

Welcome to the Temple of Pentacles, the domain of the earth
goddess Danu. In this temple, you will learn what it means to
be physical, to live in a flesh-and-bones body that feels, breathes,
and moves. This body, this physical vessel, is also surrounded by a
physical landscape made of wind, air, water, and, of course, earth.
Your physicality is connected to the physical nature around you.
From the sway of wildflowers, to the harsh dust storms, what
happens in your environment affects, shapes, and connects you
to something much bigger than yourself. Goddess Danu will
teach you to connect to this physical aspect of who you are,
as most are not one with their bodies; most people feel sepa-
rated from space, having forgotten that the landscape and the
self are one and the same. Just the act of taking a breath—the

very intuitive thing that keeps you tethered to the world of the physical—is difficult, shallow, and without connection for most people. When was the last time you took a breath and felt it? Did you notice how it hit the back of your throat, expanded your abdomen, and then left through your nose? Did you feel the very physical aspect of what breathing is? Maybe you did, but more than likely you generally do not. For most people, the body and its physical nature are railed against—battled, tamed, and controlled. In the conventional view, the body is never the right shape, size, fitness level, or desired appearance. Yet goddess Danu sees everything physical as a miracle, a spectacular expression of creation that can be felt, touched, loved, and enjoyed.

The Invitation: Accepting the Gift of Earth– Ace of Pentacles

You stand at the edge of the woods. The sun is gently caressing your skin, and the wind seems to whisper your name as it blows softly across your face. The woodland grass sways as if saying hello, and the wildflowers all turn their petals out as if to honor your presence. You place one foot on the path leading away from the noise and hustle of the town behind your back and make a decision to take a walk to clear your head. It only takes a few minutes for the noise to fade away and be overtaken by the song of birds. A melody carries through the trees as the wind continues to whisper your name, calling you further along the path. The light around you starts to become dappled as the leaves of the trees bend over you in a protective arch. It is almost as if this wood has been expecting you, waiting for the day you would find the path and step upon it.

The air shifts and you notice it has become much cooler, though not uncomfortably so; with less sunlight hitting your skin, you notice the drop in temperature. The path winds through a pair of ancient oak trees. You marvel at their size and place a hand on each as you pass through the narrow gap of the path. You feel the energy of the trees through the palms of your hands; it is warm and buzzing. You pause briefly at this spot, resting your fingers on their bark, soaking up this lovely feeling of connectedness, a feeling you haven't had for a very long time. You allow yourself a couple of seconds more with the trees before you put one foot in front of the other and continue on along the path. As you move beyond the two oak trees, you notice the woods have gotten darker as more trees spread their limbs and cover you, making you feel safe and protected.

Up ahead you hear music unlike the melody of the birds—it's as if someone is having a party. As you get closer, you hear the merriment and see shadows dancing along the ground. You become cautious about approaching without knowing who or what is up ahead. You look to see if there is somewhere else to walk—perhaps another path—but find you have come to the edge of a clearing, as if the woods around you have opened up into a large arena. The path you were on makes its way through the center of the clearing to a large standing stone. You can still hear the music and the low hum of voices. Shadows seem to dance around the standing stone, but you don't see anyone else. You leave the safety of the trees and continue on the path, making your way to its destination. As you get closer, you see the standing stone has elaborate markings and carvings all over its surface, as if depicting a story—though not a story you can seem to figure out. The shadows around the standing stone seem to part as you get closer to the center, moving away from the path as if to offer you passage to your final stop along your journey. You instinctively raise your right hand and place it on the giant spiral carved into the stone before you. As the skin of your palm makes contact with the cool surface of the stone, you take a deep and cleansing breath. You close your eyes as you start to feel the stone's pulsing energy through your fingertips. You take another few deep breaths and open your eyes.

Standing beside you is a woman with hair the color of river mud, long and flowing around her, contained only by a band of carved wood that sits atop her head like a small, unassuming crown. Her blue robes cascade around her like water gently flowing over rocks. Her earth-colored eyes look deep into you as if seeing past your physical body and into your soul. She smiles and holds out her hand in offering. Removing your right hand from the standing stone, you reach out to touch her in greeting. As your skin makes contact, the space around you comes to life. Where there were once only shadows is now filled with the most dazzling array of Fae folk you have ever seen.

The music is loud and clear now, and the sight and sounds of revelers fill your senses; everything seems brighter and richer in color than it was before. Even your sense of smell and hearing seem to be amplified. It is as if someone turned the dial up on your senses and gave you superhero capabilities. The woman beside you continues to hold your hand and smile. You begin to speak but she gives a sharp shake of her head. She reaches inside the folds of fabric which you can see now are a dress wrapped in a deep blue cape. She pulls out a single golden coin. You turn your hand over; she places it in your palm and closes your fingers around it. For the first time since you entered the clearing, she speaks.

"Do you accept this gift?"

Once again she looks deep into your eyes, awaiting your response. The intensity of her gaze makes you feel there is more to what is being offered than a simple coin. You take a breath and steady yourself before you respond.

"Yes, I accept this gift." The words leave your mouth before you have a chance to think about them further.

The woman before you nods and removes her hand from your fist. You open your hand and pick up the coin, taking a good look at it for the first time. On one side is a pentagram carved elegantly into the metal, decorated with flowers and twigs. On the other side is a triangle shape made of three spirals. Just like the standing stone, you notice this coin seems to have its own energy as it pulses slightly on your palm. Closing your fingers around the coin, you lift your head to thank the woman, only to find you are standing alone in the clearing once more. Shadows dance at your feet; as you look down, you see the path has extended itself and continues on through the clearing. You lean against the standing stone, trying to make sense of what just happened. Where did the woman and the revelers go?

How can a space that was only moments ago filled with life and light—so bright and so intense—just vanish?

You realize you have a choice to make: you can either go back the way you came and take the coin with you as a reminder of this strange yet wonderful interaction, or you can continue on along the path. You start to play with the coin, flipping it around your fingers. Looking at the coin, you decide to leave your decision to fate and make a mental deal with yourself. If the coin lands with the pentagram facing up, you will go back the way you came and leave this place. If, however, the triple spiral triangle lands facing up, you will continue along the path and see where it leads. You take a deep, centering breath and flip the coin, catching it in your hand and flipping it over onto the top of your other hand. Slowly you remove your hand to see what the coin has decided for you and let out a sigh of relief as you stare down at the triple spiral triangle that beams back up at you. Keeping the coin in your hand, you turn and place your feet back once more upon the path, facing the woods that would have taken you back to where you started. You acknowledge that where you have been holds little interest compared to the excitement of what awaits. Turning around, you reach out and touch the standing stone one last time and bow your head as if in silent prayer. With the coin in your hand and a smile on your face, you start walking across the clearing with playful energy, away from the safety and protection of the woods and toward the unknown.

Devotional Exercise
The goddess has bestowed upon you a gift, one that you willingly accepted. This is in and of itself usually the only lesson we need to learn here in the Ace: accepting a gift and all the conditions that come with it. Yet most people would just like to take the coin and run. The goddess teaches us that there is always an exchange of energy; somehow, we always give back that which we have received, in multiple ways, in thousands of exchanges over our lifetime. There is no such thing as taking and never giving back, as the universe is always restoring karmic balance in one form or another. The real lesson of the Ace of Pentacles is to know exactly *how* you will give back—do not be at the mercy of karmic laws. Instead, be empowered and inspired by

the generous goddess who gave to you without thinking twice because she knew you would be a worthy investment.

The biggest gift the goddess gives you through the Ace of Pentacles is your physical body. It is a blessing that comes with its own karma and needs to be of service. How we honor this gift will set the tone for how we honor all gifts that come into our life. When we took on our physical form, we took the coin of life from the goddess, who in turn gifted us flesh, bone, and blood along with a mind, senses, and emotions. All of these things are a deeply divine and sacred gift; here, as an act of devotion, it is time to give thanks and find a way to give back to the goddess through your physical body.

Remove the Ace of Pentacles from your deck and place it in front of you where you can see it. Now get your journal and a pen and write a letter of thanks to the Ace of Pentacles for your body and everything it allows you to do here on the physical plane. You could write about anything from celebrating your tastebuds, to thanking your body for the experience of creating life and giving birth. It might be a blessing that your body is mobile and allows you to travel, walk, explore, hike. Perhaps now is the perfect time to give thanks to your health and all the things that health allows you to do.

Start your journal letter with the following sentence: "Dear Ace of Pentacles, I humbly give thanks for the following gifts the goddess has bestowed upon me." Now you can either make a gratitude list or keep writing in letter form. Once you are complete and feel as though you cannot write any more, end it as follows: "Last but not least, I give thanks to you, Ace of Pentacles, as you are the reminder that the goddess has blessed me with this physical journey. When I see you appear in my life, I know I am being asked to count the blessings you and the goddess have bestowed upon me." Once your letter is complete, take it and your Ace of Pentacles card to your altar, light a candle, grab your favorite crystal, and dab on some essential oil. Read your letter out loud. When you have finished reading it, place it inside a jar or glass with your card and leave it on your altar for twenty-four hours. Blow the candle out once you are finished if it is not safe to leave it burning.

Stepping into the Circle: Boundaries and Holding Sacred Space– Two, Three, and Four of Pentacles

You walk along the path for what feels like hours. Having left the clearing behind, you now make your way through what appears to be a wild meadow filled with flowers, bees, and butterflies. The path meanders its way gently through this wildlife wonderland, and every so often a scent of one of the flower patches makes its way to you on a gentle breeze. So far, you have heard no noises from the outside world—no other people, no cars, no signs of human life appear to be anywhere. A part of you feels a sense of relief to have found somewhere you can be totally alone, but another part of you is wondering how long it will take you to make your way back to civilization. As these competing thoughts wage a battle inside your head, they draw your focus from the outside world and distract you. You do not notice a stone in front of you and trip over it, landing face down in the dirt. As the shock of the fall starts to fade and you become aware of your surroundings, you hear the sound of sniggering, a light laughter as you ever so slowly lift your face from the dirt. Moving up onto all fours, you pick yourself up and dust yourself off only to see two young girls sitting at the end of what appears to be a stone labyrinth.

"How does the dirt taste this time of year?" one of the girls asks as she tries and fails to compose herself.

"Like dirt," you reply, annoyed at being mocked.

The second girl walks towards you. "Forgive my sister, she finds humor in others' misfortune."

You flick your gaze between the two girls, who can't be much older than seventeen. Although one of them is still laughing at you, something feels familiar about them. The second girl snaps her fingers in front of your face.

"Hey! Come back to earth before you end up with a dust-covered tongue again."

Blinking with annoyance, you turn your gaze to her and stare deep into her mud-colored eyes.

The first girl seems to have collected herself and makes her way to stand on the other side of you. "Do you have the coin?" she asks.

You turn and face her, stunned. "How did you know … ?"

But before you can finish, the second girl waves her hand at you. "You would not have found us if Mother had not given you the coin. Show it to us and we will prepare you to enter the circle."

"The circle? You mean the labyrinth?"

The first girl rolls her eyes at you but turns to the second girl and sighs, "Every time! Why do we have to do this every time?"

The second girl responds to your question. "The circle is not a shape; it is a space … a sacred space. Only the chosen can enter the circle of Danu. The goddess herself has chosen you and deemed you worthy of entry. But first we must prepare you, starting with the coin. We don't take it; it is yours to keep."

She smiles at you and speaks to you the way you would find yourself speaking to someone you pity. You fumble around in your pockets and pull out the coin, showing it to the two girls, who seem to have gotten serious as they nod at each other. The first girl wanders off, about ten paces away from where you stand and starts picking over rocks. She decides on two and brings them back.

"Hold out your arms and open your hands," she orders you. The second girl nods and you stretch out your arms and open your hands. The first girl places the rocks in your hands. They feel too heavy, like they will fall from your grip any second.

"Close your eyes. Concentrate not on the weight of the rocks, but on finding your balance. It is not the rocks you have a problem with—it is your lack of faith in what you can hold with your own two hands."

The strain of the rocks pulls on your arms, and you feel yourself trying your best to balance them as if you are a juggler on a tightrope. You close your eyes and take a deep breath. You do your best to ignore the burning of your arm muscles and the fatigue of your hands bending under a weight you are not used to carrying. You breathe deeply again and pull yourself up tall, relaxing your shoulders, and visualize yourself as perfectly balanced, as if the weight in your grip is normal and part of you. You allow yourself to get lost in this image of yourself as balanced, strong, and capable of taking on more than you first thought possible, so much so that you don't even notice that the girls have removed the rocks from your hands and replaced them with coins, one in each palm.

"You may open your eyes and enter the circle," the two girls say in unison.

It takes you a moment to realize you are no longer holding the rocks. Your arms ache and you feel the need to shake them out like wet sheets in the breeze. Taking the two new coins, you place them in your pocket with the first as you near the mouth of the labyrinth, which seems three times bigger than when you first noticed it. You can feel a pulse coming from the path and briefly hesitate before stepping forward. You look back over your shoulder to the two girls, as if in hope that they have some instruction on how to proceed. Instead, you see they have lost interest in you and have picked up a couple of drums and are beginning to play. The first beats out a smooth, consistent beat like that of the heart, whereas the second girl seems lost in a trance of rhythmic drumming that blends with her sister's heartbeat song. You turn back to face the labyrinth and take a deep breath, wondering if you are meant to say anything before you enter, or if there is a wrong and right way to proceed. The sound of drumming catches up to you; before you can dive deeper into your mind of worry and self-doubt, you find your feet have moved on their own, moving to the rhythm of the drums, to the pull of the path. Without even knowing it, you have entered the circle. As you cross the threshold between the world outside of the labyrinth and inside on the path, another gold coin appears in the dirt right in front of your feet. You bend down to pick it up and quickly put it in your pocket along with the other three. You hold your pocket protectively for a moment. Deciding your coins are safe and protected, you proceed further into the circle, winding your way around the spiral.

Devotional Exercise

There are many times in our lives where we feel unable or unprepared to take on something new. We believe there isn't enough time, money, or support. Ironically, none of these things show up until we take our first step along the path of this new experience. The Two of Pentacles will show you how to juggle what you need, while the Three of Pentacles will bring in the missing pieces. The Four of Pentacles shows you that you have what you need but must be brave enough to let go and trust that everything is in place. This sense of trust is often how we feel when we have been blessed by the goddess in the Ace of Pentacles. We are initially excited by the gift, accepting it without too much thought about what it means to commit to something in exchange for another. In the pentacles, your exchange will be a physical one—your time, your body, or your money. The nature of the goddess's gift in the Ace will determine the form of payment being asked of you now.

Remove the Two, Three, and Four of Pentacles from your deck and line them up in a row. Pick up the rest of your deck and shuffle slowly, closing your eyes if you need to. Ask goddess Danu your first question:

What is it I already have that I can juggle to honor the gift you have bestowed upon me?

When you feel you have infused the cards with your question, select one card only and place it on top of the Two of Pentacles. Pick your deck up again and begin shuffling. This time, ask Danu:

How can I allow assistance into my life to help me embrace your gift?

When you feel the question is infused into the cards, select just one and place it on top of the Three of Pentacles. Begin shuffling your cards one last time and ask the goddess:

What step can I take to move through my self-doubt?

When you feel the question is infused in the cards, select just one card and place it on top of the Four of Pentacles. You now have an entirely new three-card spread overlaid on your original cards.

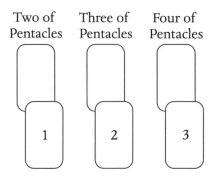

Two of Pentacles	Three of Pentacles	Four of Pentacles
1	2	3

These cards are answers straight from the goddess herself. She is giving you guidance about how to heal your body, how to increase your abundance, or how best to manage your time. Regardless of the cards you have drawn, these are your answers. Do not try to get a more pleasant or pleasing card—to the goddess, this is a slap in the face. Understand that Danu knows the workings of the physical world intimately; it is her domain, and she is constantly attending to troubles and problems that crop up in the world of material and physical things. Place your cards on your altar and leave them there until you feel you have worked through each answer. You will walk these cards much the same way you walked the labyrinth: slowly, deliberately, and with your five senses wide open. As you work through each card, make sure to lay an offering of thanks on your altar along with a small prayer of gratitude. When all three cards have been walked, remove them and move on to the next section.

Bound, Unbound, and Healing the Wounds: Five, Six, and Seven of Pentacles

You stand in the middle of the labyrinth, wrapping your arms around yourself, as the wind seems to have picked up. A cold and unrelenting gale whips around you and there is nowhere to find shelter. The tree line is miles away and there are no buildings in this clearing. You pull your arms tighter and tighter around you as you stand in the middle of the labyrinth. Dust starts to swirl, so you bend your head to protect your eyes. The wind picks up even more, and you realize that there is no way you can fully protect yourself or your body completely, despite your best efforts. You crouch down, making yourself as small as possible, doing the best you can to weather this sudden storm. Shielding your eyes, you try to peer through the flying dust and wind, but visibility is almost at zero. Suddenly you feel very alone and exceedingly helpless.

Contracting your energy and your body, you sink into yourself, your mind races, and all the old negative chatter starts to scream inside your head. Let's face it—you have no idea where you are, no one knows where you are, and now you have no idea how to get back to where you started. You are stuck, at the mercy of the "right now," which is unpleasant, uncomfortable, and a little terrifying. As you crouch in the dirt to make yourself as small as possible, you think about all the other mistakes you have made and all the times you followed your gut but it ended in disaster. Your past failings swirl inside your mind, echoing the storm you are trying desperately to shelter from. You become so caught up in the raging of your mind that you don't notice that the wind has died away—the dust has settled and someone is standing before you, offering a hand of assistance.

Slowly but surely, your awareness comes back to you and you notice the woman with the mud-colored hair standing before you. Her eyes are sparkling, and she has a soft and gentle expression on her face. She extends a hand to help you to your feet. You reach out and willingly accept her assistance. Your legs are a little jellylike, so the woman leans in so you can use her body for support. You reach down to dust yourself off, becoming more and more aware of the world around you once again. You notice that you are no longer in the middle of the labyrinth and in fact are no longer in a field at all—instead, you find yourself in the center of a village. People are moving around you, children are laughing, and dogs are barking. You start to wonder if you blacked out in the storm and are now having a *Wizard of Oz* moment.

"Come," the woman says as she turns and heads toward a small shop front. You notice the sign over the door reads "Unbound Healing." You rub the last of the dust off your face, leaving smudges across your cheeks, and follow the woman into the store. Once in the store, a woman dressed in a deep green flowing dress with flaming red hair offers you a warm cloth and directs you to the restroom. You close the door behind you and lock it, settling your gaze on your reflection in the mirror. You take a look at yourself for the first time since you followed the path through the woods. You look like you have been spat out of a hurricane! Taking a deep breath, you loosen your shoulders and only just become aware of how tight your entire body has been. You begin to wash the dirt off your face. Next to the taps are a hair brush and what looks like an essential oil spray. Hanging on the peg next to the basin is a change of clothes with your name pinned to them.

You finish cleaning yourself off, brush your hair out and mist it with the spray, and change into the clean clothes which are, of course, a perfect fit. You study yourself in the mirror and realize you look different. You are standing a little taller, even though your body is aching from having contracted itself so tightly. Your eyes have a sparkle to them that you never noticed previously, and you have no idea what was in that spray bottle, but your hair is shining in a way it hasn't in a very long time. There is a knock on the door and you hear your name being softly spoken. Feeling ready to face whatever happens next, you unlock the door and open it slowly.

"Oh, you found the clean clothes. Excellent. Come, come. My sister awaits you."

You follow the woman with a quick nod of the head. At this point, you have decided it might be best to just go with things and see what happens. You figure that at least you aren't alone, and everyone you have encountered thus far seems to want to help you, even though they do not know you and you still have no idea where you are or who these women are.

"Oh—"the woman turns to face you—"I forgot, these are yours." She reaches into her pocket and pulls out six gold coins, which she hands to you.

You look at the coins for a moment, unsure whether to take them or not.

"Go on." She nudges them forward. "Take them. They are yours, after all. You have earned them." Smiling, she takes your hand and places the coins in it, closing your fingers around the cold metal. Her arm drops away and you come to a door. She knocks and you hear the faint murmur of a voice on the other side. She opens the door and says to you, "Okay, here you are. Go right in—my sister will be right with you."

You step up to the door and can't believe what you are seeing: Beyond the threshold is one of the most beautiful garden you have ever seen. Right in the middle of it, under a golden lacework gazebo, is a healing bed covered in blankets and pillows. Beside it, in the same robes as the woman with mud-colored hair is a short woman whose long flaxen hair hangs in tight curls down her back, making her appear even shorter as she moves around near what appears to be a counter of some kind. She finally turns and faces you, her face lined heavily with time. And yet, her body moves with the flex of someone much younger.

"Come, come." She pats the healing bed and motions for you to move forward. "It is okay, child; you are safe here. Please lie upon the bed."

Your gaze drifts over the bed; it *does* look warm and comfortable, and you really could use a bit of a lie-down if you are being honest. You shrug and climb up onto the bed, laying your head down onto the softest pillow you have rested your head upon. There is heat radiating up from the bed itself into your back, and slowly you start to feel all the contracted muscles relax along your spine. You release a sigh of both pain and relief as you let go of the last of the tension around your shoulders. The woman places her hand above your forehead and heat flows from the palm of her hand across your face, relaxing you even more. As you sink deeper into this healing warmth, you become more and more aware of the sounds of birds and the buzzing of bees. It is as if the volume inside the garden has been turned up. The scents of the flowers and the trees also start to permeate your senses—pine, lavender, rose, and so many other glorious scents wash over you like a wave. The woman taps the top of your head and whispers the word "sleep." You close your eyes as your consciousness drifts away.

Devotional Exercise

When we start to make significant changes within ourselves, the outside world of physical people and material things starts to shift as well, though often not at all in the way we had hoped. At this stage of your transformation, it can actually feel like you are going backward, not forward: your bank accounts can start to shrink at a very rapid rate, you can become sick, you can lose friends or even feel shut out from the life you used to live. Instead of feeling like you belong, you feel like an outsider to your own life. Your life will become the Five of Pentacles at this stage of the process. Here is where most people give up and decide that maybe what they had wasn't that bad after all, as working with the Five of Pentacles can be difficult. However, a few people like yourself understand that you are being asked to take an observer's point of view of your life. Everything that previously bound you has some separation to it that can now be examined.

Change can't happen when things stay the same—some things must go or be left behind so new things can make their way to you through the Six and Seven of Pentacles. What happens here is an identification process that allows you to see what has restricted you. From there, you can take the steps to unbind yourself to begin the healing process. And because we are dealing with pentacles, all of this—healing, letting go, change—is about your physical experience, including your physical body. The goddess knows that this phase of the journey can be difficult, but she also wants you to understand how necessary it will be to your priestess work. You will need to have walked this stage yourself before you can hold a sacred circle for someone else going through it. You need to be able to identify the stages and moments of progression this stage brings, from the Five to the awaiting assistance in the Six into the healing phase of the Seven of Pentacles.

Cord Cutting and Healing

To begin this exercise, take your Five of Pentacles out of your deck and place it in front of you. As you look at this card, what is the very first thing that comes to mind when you think of leaving your old life behind for something new? Whatever it is, write it down, but don't think too hard about it. Trust that whatever has popped into your head is correct. Next, pick up your deck of cards (leaving the Five of Pentacles out) upright and in front of you. Hold your deck to your heart and take a nice deep breath. Now ask the following question to Danu aloud:

"What am I really afraid of?"

When you are ready, shuffle your deck, fan the cards out facing down, and select just one card. Place it on top of the Five of Pentacles. The card you have selected is going to be the very issue you are going to pull an energy cord from—there is an energetic attachment to this fear that must be surrendered to the goddess, allowing you to move through your priestess journey with fresh eyes and restored hope. Take a moment to journal with the card and the fear that first popped into your head. When you feel you are done, put your pen down.

Keeping the two tarot cards in front of you, place your hands over them and take a few deep breaths as you say the following:

"Mother Danu, I surrender this fear to you. I offer it back; I do not need to carry its burden with me any longer."

Keeping your hands on the cards, notice where in your body you feel this attachment. You might feel a pull or tug, a hot or cold spot, or perhaps tightness somewhere in your body. This is where the cord of this fear needs to be removed. If you need to, close your eyes to visualize yourself gently pulling this cord free from your body. If you can do it with your eyes open, that is fine as well. As you slowly and lovingly remove the cord, notice what it looks and feels like. Is it dried and withered or thick and sticky? Also notice if the cord easily came away in your hands or if it was harder to remove. Just keep a mental note in case you wish to journal about it more once you have finished this exercise.

Now that the cord is released, recite this small prayer out loud:

> I thank the fear and I lovingly release it and all who played a part in keeping it attached to me. Mother, Goddess, Danu, I give this cord to you. Take it and return it to the vortex from which its energy came. I open myself up now, Mother, to all good that this fear was blocking or keeping any from me. I surrender this to you. In love, as one, thank you. And so it is.

Now it is time to allow yourself the gift of healing. Pick your deck of cards up again and remove the Six and Seven of Pentacles. Take these cards to your altar and set them up along with any crystals, stones, flowers, leaves, or other offerings to the goddess along with a white, green, or pink candle. Make sure you have some salt on your altar as well; we are setting a healing space, so a nice piece of Himalayan rock salt will do the trick.

I have a very small packet of Hawaiian rock salt given to me as a gift on my healing altar. The salt sets up a nice protective barrier around your work and helps hold your altar's energy.

Once your altar is set up and arranged in the way you want it for your healing session, light your candle. Settle yourself into a nice comfortable position, making sure you can see your Six and Seven of Pentacles cards. Rub your hands together to activate the small chakras in the palms and then place your hands over the area from which you removed the cord. If this area is not easily accessible on your body, then rest your hands as close to it as possible while visualizing the space on your body so the energy has a target. Say the following out loud while looking at your tarot cards:

> "I open myself to receive the gift the Six of Pentacles is offering me."

Take a nice deep breath and repeat again,

> "I open myself to receive the gift the Six of Pentacles is offering me."

Take another deep breath and repeat one last time,

> "I open myself to receive the gift the Six of Pentacles is offering me.

Take another nice deep breath, keeping your hands over your body. Close your eyes for a few minutes while the energy moves through your hands into the area you plucked the cord from, remaining as open as possible while the Six of Pentacles flows through you. When you feel done (which might mean your hands go cold, you notice the energy has turned itself off, or you just can't focus anymore), remove your hands and place them in a prayer position as you thank the goddess and the cards for their healing.

To end your session, say the following small prayer:

> Goddess, Mother, Molder of lives, Miracle-maker,
> Danu, thank you for this healing. I shall be at one
> with the Seven of Pentacles as I surrender to the
> role of the observer, watching in wonder as your
> miracles blossom and bloom in me, around me,
> and through me. And so it is.

You can either blow the candle out at this point or keep it burning if it is safe to do so.

To wrap this exercise up, spend some time with your journal and make as many notes as you wish about anything that came up for you during the healing session or even if you feel different. Perhaps your thoughts seem more positive and your head feels lighter. Don't forget to clean your altar and give all of the natural elements you used during your session back to the goddess in the form of ashes, compost, or scattering them around your garden.

Gifts of the Scar: Eight and Nine of Pentacles

You find yourself having the most amazing dream—it feels very much like every wish you have ever made has suddenly become real. Your body has no hint of pain, your mind is clear, and you feel more energy flowing through your body than you ever have before. You feel like you could conquer the world. Like nothing is impossible and all can be done given the right amount of time, and the right amount of preparation. In your dream you see yourself at your optimal best—in the flow and everything just magically falling into place around you. This is a feeling you could get used to. Somewhere off in the distance you hear a voice, yet it is so faint you have to strain to really hear the words. *"Take a mental picture and remember how this moment feels."* You do your very best to take a snapshot of the dream scene playing out in your mind's eye. It is such a beautiful vision and you really don't want to lose it. You make the colors extra vibrant and get as close up as you can on the scene. You want to make sure you are imprinting every aspect of this moment into your subconscious memory.

The dream shows the life you have always known you deserve, the feeling you have been working so hard to feel. It has the energy you want to be in the flow of every second of every day, no matter what the rest of the world throws your way. You soak up this image in all of its richness, snapping the final shot and saving it in your memory, though not so deep that you cannot access it on command. Now you notice the edges are starting to fray; the dreamscape is dissolving and dissipating like a clearing smoke. You can hear noises from outside the dream that you could not hear before. You know before your conscious mind sneaks back in that the dream is over. You feel the heat of the hands above your third eye. You notice the scent of incense as it comes with each inhale through your nose. You feel the weight of your body and know that you are once more on the healing bed, in the room with the women whose names you still don't know.

You feel lighter, clearer, and more alert and attentive than before. It feels like a weight has been lifted from you: a past pain that you can no longer locate. But more to the point, you don't want to locate it. The best part is that you feel a spark of joy, a sense of achievement that you have never felt before. You have no idea where it has come from but you know life right now seems to be more of a gift than a burden. The woman removes her hands from your forehead and gently touches the side of your arm. She indicates that when you are ready, you may sit up and move to retrieve a glass of water she is holding. Rising slowly, you know that when you get off this table, you won't be the same person you were when you got on it. You are elevated in a way even you can't yet fully comprehend. But you know. Things in your life won't be the same from here on in. There is no going back, only forward. The past is nothing but a scar, and from it you will move into an unknown future with confidence, resilience, and grace.

Devotional Exercise

All healing leaves scars. Some can be seen and others only we can find and admire. The trouble with scars is not that they exist but the energy they tend to collect. All our scars, internal and external, have an energy vortex all their own. They hold stories—or more to the point, they keep stories trapped, frozen in time, and encoded into the body. And unfortunately, it's all too often that these stories are not the type we want to keep telling. The good news is that you can change that story, and with it, the energy that pumps through your scars. The Eight of Pentacles often talks about rewards that come from a level of achievement through work. That said, this work doesn't always have to be physical in nature or even related to a job; it can also refer to things like healing. Let's face it—some of the hardest work you will do is healing, and the goddess knows this. It is why she provides these sacred spaces for you to collect a different type of payment, a more empowered source of karmic income. You could even call them "karma coins." The goddess knows that you have come into this plane of contrast to expand your well of desire. She also understands you may have beaten yourself up a bit while you worked out what you wanted and what you didn't. But now that you understand that you are the powerful creator of your experience, it is time to get every cell in your body dancing to the beat of a new vibration. Burn the karmic scars and collect the new karma coins!

In the following exercise, you will want to burn the karma from one of your scars and fill it up with your karma coins. Remove your Eight and Nine of Pentacles cards from your deck. The Eight is going to be your burning karma card. What does "burning karma" mean, and how do you do it? It means breaking the patterns or habits that keep you in a state of suffering. The Eight of Pentacles is the card of hard work—and it *is* hard work to leave habits behind, even if they no longer serve you. You may have a physical scar that you wish to do this exercise with, or an emotional one, but the process is the same.

Settle into a comfy chair, yoga pose, or you could even lie down on your bed (don't worry, you will not be going to sleep). If you are working on burning the karma from a physical scar, place your hand or fingers on it. If it is an emotional scar, use your hands to scan your body and see where you feel something when you think of this scar, as this is where the energy is trapped in your body, the karmic loop. Once you have found your scar, close your eyes and take a deep, slow breath, feeling the breath flow all the way out of your fingertips and into your scar. As the breath continues to flow from the tips of your fingers, see it turn into flames and burn through the glob of energy that is your stuck, habitual karma. As it burns, listen for any messages and notice if you feel any resistance to releasing this energy trapped around and woven into your scar. Watch in your mind's eye as the people, places, and situations burn away with your touch, dissolving into ashes and blowing away from the breeze of your breath. When you feel complete, or you have done all you feel capable of doing today, remove your fingers from your scar and shake out your hand. Flick all the energy off of it. Open your eyes and sit up.

Now remove the Nine of Pentacles from your deck, as this is the card we are going to use to recode and reset your scar with karma coins, which we can think of as good karma that gets stored up to be used or shared whenever you wish. It is like storing away wishes and blessings inside your body. In this case, you are going to fill your scar with nine karma coins, nine blessings ready to burst forth and grow when the time and conditions are right. Once you have your card in front of you, place your fingers on the spot where your scar is. This time, you are going to keep your eyes open and focused on the Nine of Pentacles card. As you breathe, imagine nine gold coins leaping out of your card and into your scar. See them do so one at a time, sparkling with promises, illuminated from the inside out with divine potential, radiating with love. Each karma coin brings with it luck, magic, success, prosperity and, of course, healing. Breathe slowly and deeply as you reset and recode your scar.

Take your time. Don't rush. Let those coins slowly and gently flow into you, one by one. Once all nine pentacles/karma coins are infused within your scar, stay with this energy for a few minutes and watch this new karma spread all over your body, from the top of your head to the tips of your toes. Perhaps you see it as light, or maybe it has a well-defined color and texture to it. Just remember to breathe deep and slow. Allow the new energy in. You can remove your fingers from your body and just relax into the breath, closing your eyes if you wish. Stay with this energy for a few minutes before you end your session.

Once you are done, place the two cards on your altar and give an offering to Danu. Say a prayer to her, light a green healing candle, and give thanks. You can do this under a first or last quarter moon if you want to amplify the power of the prayer and healing, but it isn't necessary. When you are finished with your healing and altar work, cleanse the cards by putting them on a salt or selenite brick or by waving them under the smoke of an herb wand before you put them back into your deck.

Leaving the Circle and Moving On: Ten of Pentacles

As you leave the healing room and say goodbye to the wonderful woman who facilitated your healing work, you embrace her in a way you have never embraced anyone before. She is warm and holds you firmly yet lovingly. You exchange your final goodbyes and head out. The sun blinds you temporarily but then you see her—Danu is waiting for you. She doesn't call you or ask you to hurry up. She merely acknowledges you and holds your gaze, her mud-colored eyes steady, so sure and inviting. It is impossible to look away from her. So you make your way towards her. You know by her presence that it's time to say goodbye to the Temple of Pentacles. Your journey here is now complete, and it is time to move on. She is there to mark the ending of one journey and the beginning of another. As you get closer to her, the scene around you starts to dissolve and you find yourself back in the place you began, at the standing stone. And yet you are not the same as you were when you first came here. You have moved vibrational mountains. You feel more connected to the world around you and even more connected to your body. Not to mention how much more aware you are of how your inner world creates your outer experience.

The goddess holds out her hand. You hold on to it as she guides you out of the circle and moves you back to the path that leads away from the temple, away from the standing stone and away from her. You reach inside your pocket to find you now have ten coins; you hold them out to her as if in offering, but she declines and indicates that you have earned them. You place them back into your pocket yet don't move your feet. You know it's time to go but that doesn't mean you feel ready. As if sensing your resistance to turn and walk away, the goddess recites an incantation that is barely audible. As she does so, the winds pick up once again. Dust swirls around, limiting your visibility. You lose sight of the temple, the goddess, and the standing stone.

Just as quickly as it began, the dust storm clears, dropping to the ground like rain made of earth and stone. All you see in front of you now is a wall. It is so tall that you would never be able to climb it, and it seems to be spread as far as your eyes can see in either direction. Your lips smile, but your heart aches just a little, because you understand this is the goddess's way of letting you know that this path can no longer be traveled. When you see her again, it will be on a different path, on a different journey. You put your hands in your pocket and jingle your coins, feeling their coolness as they clank around in your pocket. You turn away from the wall and head back along the path; it is the only way you can go forward.

Devotional Exercise

This exercise should be done during a new moon, when the moon has come full circle and is in the vibration of both ending and a new beginning. The darkness of the new moon gives you the space to reflect on the journey you have taken as well as time to think about how you want to proceed once the light begins its return. For this, you are going to set up a new moon altar, and you are going to need to place the following items upon it: your Ten of Pentacles tarot card, a printed-out picture of the goddess Danu, ten coins of your choice, and a silver candle. You can add anything else you wish, but make sure the listed items here are included, as they are necessary.

This will be your closing ceremony for the goddess, a way of honoring her and saying thank you for the gifts she has bestowed upon you while you walked in her Temple of Pentacles. Each of the ten coins you are placing on your altar represents ten gifts the goddess has given you or you are expecting her to give you. Perhaps she has gifted you with health. Speak it into the coin and place it on your altar. Since you have been in the Pentacles' temple, maybe you have been given the gift of a raise, promotion, or won a prize: speak it into the coin and place it on your altar. You may have even been gifted with a new mindset relating to health, well-being, and abundance. Whatever it is, speak it into your coin and place it on your altar. Do this until all ten coins have been filled with your gifts and placed on the altar with Danu.

Once your coins are placed, light some sage or other cleansing herbs and wave the smoke over your altar to set it for your prayer and honoring work. Now, light your silver candle and repeat the following closing prayer:

> *Goddess, thank you for walking with me*
>
> *Thank you for sharing your gifts*
>
> *To you I give this prayer*
>
> *To you I give thanks*

I know now I do not walk this physical path alone

You shadow my footsteps

Guide me with hands

Slowly but surely you nudge and redirect

Never letting me stray

Always steering me in the right direction

Goddess, I bow down to thee

Your kindness and compassion

Is the true gift

Although I leave this temple for now

Your presence will stay with me

I know you can be found

For in each step

There you will be

Blessings, dear Goddess

From my heart to yours

I am humble

I am bold

I am forever grateful

As I now close this door

And so it is.

Once you have said your prayer, you can either blow out the candle or leave it burning as long as it is safe to do so. Leave the altar until the new moon cycle has finished and then carry your ten coins with you in your purse, hand bag, or wallet as reminders of the goddess's gifts.

Chapter Six

THE TEMPLE OF SWORDS

**Truth, Knowledge, and Light:
Priestessing with Saraswati**

⟩ ⟩ ● ⟨ ⟨

Ode to Saraswati

Bells jingle as she walks

Softly but surely across the landscape

Erect, strong, and self-assured

The goddess never waivers

Never drops that which she carries

Balanced in all she does

Mind over matter

Or is it matter over mind

The center of all creation

The center of all illusion

The sands of reality constantly shift

Depending on where you direct it

The goddess knows

She understands

Each step is a song

A jingling reminder

Of the beats the mind creates

The swords are reminders

Suffering or liberation

It depends which side of the blade you use

The goddess knows where to cut

Where to slice

How to swing the blade

Graceful strokes as she wanders on

The sound at her feet

Jingle jingle the bells to chime

Enter her temple

The time has come

Pick up your sword

Sharpen your mind

The lesson has already begun.

Introduction to the Temple of Swords

Welcome to the Temple of Swords, domain of the goddess Saraswati. Here in this temple, you will learn what it means to be of one mind—to create with one mind and engage in a world with single-minded thought. You will learn how to be mentally strong, how to guard your thoughts, and how to be flexible with your thinking. Goddess Saraswati will teach you how to focus and how to leverage your mind and expand your awareness. She will show you where you need a mental workout and where your mental muscles are their strongest. Oftentimes her technique may seem somewhat unorthodox, but her lessons are always true. In the Temple of Swords, you will begin to understand that you are what you think and what you think creates what kind of world you will experience. Mindfulness, awareness, and consciousness are the key lessons this temple offers. If you pick up the sword, you are accepting this goddess's lesson, of mind and of self. Watch your thoughts, for they can cut. Be careful what you focus on, as it might appear in front of you. Step lightly upon your beliefs, as they may not be as stable as you wish them to be. Not much is real in the realm of the mind, so be on the lookout for illusions, tricks, and sleights of hand. The goddess knows this is why you must practice and why you have entered her temple. To master the illusion, expand your reality and push the limits of your consciousness. Cross the threshold if you dare, and see if you are worthy of Saraswati's sword.

The Invitation: Accepting the Gift of Air–Ace of Swords

The air is clean and clear, and now that you have spent time in the Temple of Pentacles, you have come to appreciate the sacred act of breathing. You take a deep breath and feel the air move down your throat and into your lungs. As you breathe you notice everything around you seems to exhale with you. The leaves on the trees begin to rustle, the wildflowers bend and sway, and the slightest of breezes tickles the end of your nose. You feel a connection to the land and your body like you have never experienced before. All your senses feel sharpened. Everything looks brighter, more vibrant. The scent of the forest relaxes you, and the sound of beautiful music dances in your ears. The music is unlike any other you have ever heard before. It is strange yet familiar all at once. You close your eyes and just listen, focusing on only the music as you turn your body like a compass to work out what direction it appears to be coming from. Once you have located it, you start making your way toward it, taking you off the path and deeper into the forest.

The only guide you have are the notes floating through the woods that bounce off the bark. The terrain starts to become rocky, but you know you are headed in the right direction—the music is getting louder. You find you have to scramble over rocks as you now climb up what seems like a mountain. The tree line starts to recede behind you as you climb even further. As you come to a ledge, you notice a small but well-worn path that seems to go around the side of the mountain. You set your feet firmly on it and follow it. Out of nowhere, you find yourself in a valley-like clearing. Sitting there on a log is a beautiful woman beside a lake, playing an instrument that from this distance looks like an elongated banjo.

The woman's long black hair wraps around her shoulders like a protective blanket. It has the most incredible pink flowers threaded through it. Her feet are bare except for the delicate gold chains that chime and tinkle as she taps her foot in time to her music. Her skin glows golden-brown in the sunlight and gold bangles adorn her arms. She wears an orange top that reveals her midriff and a sheer pearl-colored skirt with perfectly round pearls stitched into the hem with matching leggings underneath. From your vantage point, it seems like this woman is glowing—a

radiant light seems to beam from her entire body. She stops playing and raises her head, deeply looking you in the eye.

"Come here, child. Come sit with me."

You move off the path and into the clearing. As you do, you
notice that all other sound has ceased—the loudest thing you
can hear is your breathing. Maybe the trek up the rocks was
more strenuous than you thought. You approach the place
where the woman is sitting. She rests her instrument by her
side, and as you get closer you can see it is not a banjo at all,
but you are still no wiser to what it actually is. It has beautiful
gold patterns that run over its face and up its neck. If you had
not heard it being played, you would have thought it was more
a piece of art than something that can be used. As you draw
closer to the woman, she gestures for you to sit just in front of
her on a smooth boulder. You expect the rock to be hard and
cool, but notice it is, instead, warm and feels like it gently gives
under your weight, offering you comfort and support.

"You have question marks in your eyes," the woman says
through a grin, never once letting her soft brown eyes leave
your gaze. "Yet I think you do not hear the answers. Your mind
is so loud it has scared away all the birds."

Laughing, she stands and makes her way to where you are
sitting. She seems to almost float as she walks. Her jingling
anklets are the only indication that she is moving her legs at all.
The closer she gets to you, the more noise you can hear. And
what you hear sounds like a raging river mixed with a very loud
crowd. With each step she takes, the volume increases. Now
as she stands in front of you, the noise is so loud you cover
your ears, yet that only seems to make everything louder. The
woman places her hands over your ears; her touch has radiant
heat that has an automatic calming effect on you.

"The noise you hear is inside you; it is your choir of inner voices all out of tune, all fighting to be heard. This is why the answers you seek are very seldom heard."

She closes her eyes, keeping her hands over your ears and takes nice deep breaths. Like magic, the noise suddenly stops. She removes her hands, opens her eyes, and smiles at you. She reaches behind her and pulls an ornate sword out of its holster.

"Your mind is like this sword. It cuts both ways. One side of the blade will bring you peace, flow, and joy. The other will bring you noise, chaos, and suffering. You must learn how to use the sword in a way that benefits you."

The sun glints off the blade as the woman moves it around like a dancer, as if she and the sword are one. When finished, she lays the sword across her palms and offers it to you.

"I offer you an invitation to the Temple of Swords. By accepting this gift, you acknowledge that you have much to learn and that the path ahead will not necessarily be easy. But if it is peace you seek, the sword can give it to you."

You take a nice deep breath and reach your hand out to touch the sword. You run your fingers over the ornate pattern along the hilt. You watch as the light dances on the highly polished metal. Then you catch your reflection in the blade and a word floats to your mind: "Accept." You stand and lay your hands out in the same way as the woman in front of you and say, "I accept."

With that, she gently places the sword in your hands, and you almost drop it, as the weight of it is so unexpected. How did this small, dainty woman in front you make this thing seem as light as a feather? The woman laughs once more.

"The more you work with it, the lighter it will become. Come, we have much work to do."

Devotional Exercise

The Ace of Swords invites you to learn more about your mind—how it thinks, what it believes, and what it holds on to. This card offers you the opportunity to change your life, bring all of your dreams to life, and cut away all of your doubts and fears. Remove this card from your deck and place it in front of you. Examine the card, allowing your eyes to soak up all the details. Is your sword pointing up to the sky, or down to the ground? Not all swords point the same way, but the Ace you have drawn will be giving you clues to how your mind works. If it is pointing to the sky, then perhaps you like to contemplate the future, constantly seeking the answers of the universe and casting your mind out into the stars. If your sword is pointed to the ground, perhaps you are more down-to-earth with your beliefs and thinking. Your downward-pointing sword could indicate your mind works better when it has an immediate, everyday purpose to focus on. Knowing where your sword points is important, as it will give the goddess a place to start your instruction. To dig deeper, pick up your deck and shuffle. Hold the cards to your heart, close your eyes, and ask the Ace of Swords two questions:

Question one: What lessons have you come to teach me today?

Question two: What will you be cutting away today?

Take another deep breath and draw two cards, placing them under your Ace of Swords. You can pick up your journal at this point and take notes or start some journal work on your cards. You can spend as much or as little time exploring the answers the cards have provided for you; it is totally up to you.

Once you are done, take your Ace of Swords card to your altar and place it there next to a picture of goddess Saraswati.

Light a white candle in honor of her gift and her invitation to enter her temple. Sit with your hands in prayer position and close your eyes just for a few moments as you spend a moment in silent reverence, silent thanks, silent devotion. When you are done, blow your candle out. You can continue this simple act of devotion for as long as you like; I recommend at least eleven days but, if you feel moved to do so, for up to forty days. The length of time depends on how long you wish to be in the presence of the goddess and inside the Temple of Swords.

Stepping into the Circle: Boundaries and Holding Sacred Space—Two, Three, and Four of Swords

The goddess hands you another sword. "Double the weight, double the focus," she says with a smirk.

"Think of these swords as representing the two parts of your mind: one is the logical, practical, rational side. The other is the intuitive, in-the-flow-inspired side. You must learn to keep them in balance, even though you will more than likely favor one over the other."

You haven't mastered holding the first sword she gave you; now with two equally heavy swords in your hands, you struggle to keep them upright, let alone balanced. No one tells you just how heavy these damn swords are; wielding them looks so easy on TV. Your arms are starting to burn from the weight of them.

The goddess moves closer to you and helps hold your arms up. "Close your eyes and feel for the balance. Stop struggling against the easiest path."

She gently releases your arms and with your eyes closed, you settle yourself with a nice deep breath, trying to see if you can feel if there is any position that doesn't feel as heavy to you. You let the weight of the swords guide you as you begin to notice that one of them is feeling lighter than the other. You begin to open your eyes to see which of the two swords is giving you some relief, when the goddess slaps the top of your head from behind you.

"No peeking," she says as she ties a piece of silk around your eyes. Even if you did open them now, there would be nothing to see.

As your mind shifts to the blindfold, the two swords once again start to drag your arms down. Just that one slight move in thought was enough to alter the balance of the swords in your hands. Then you remember that the goddess said to "feel" your way to balance. You test a theory: while your mind was on the blindfold you were feeling frustrated. What happens to the swords if you can focus on more positive thoughts or feelings? You adjust the swords in your hands and do your best to get them as comfortable as possible. Next, you find the happiest memory you can and start to focus on it. As a grin starts to form on your lips, you notice your arms don't seem to be aching, and your muscles seem to have stopped burning from the weight of the metal in your hands.

You do your best to keep the thread but, again, the moment your mental focus slips, the weight of the swords comes back. But now you know how to correct it and how to balance the swords. You laugh as you begin to really feel your way through this problem. You take another deep breath and move your mind in the direction you want it to go. The longer you can keep it engaged with the happy, loving, and compassionate feelings, the better you can hold up the swords. The trick is holding the thread; you think that should be easy enough by now. That is, until you hear a piercing cry, a sound of so much pain and anguish—your body and mind fill with the vibration of it and you drop the swords.

"It is one thing to be able to hold the mind when working in a controlled space, but what about in the world of contrast where the environment is not peaceful or friendly?" The goddess removes the blindfold, and you quickly look around for whatever was making that distressful cry. There, lying on the edge of the lake is a swan, prostrate and lifeless. A sword sticks out of its chest and a pool of what looks like blood is flowing under its body. You look up at the goddess and then rush to the bird. You bend down and gently stroke along the side of the swan's head. Just then, out of nowhere, the swan snaps at your fingers and you turn to see the goddess dissolve into a fit of giggles. Blood starts to drip from your hand and pain begins spreading up your arm and through your mind.

"Do not mind the swan. She is a good actress, no?"

The swan, the one you thought had befallen some tragedy, waddles over to the lake's edge and enters the water. Stretching out its wings, it looks at you and makes a noise that sounds awfully like a snigger. It then submerges itself into the water, and when it surfaces, it is pure white, with no sign of the fake blood anywhere on its majestic feathers. The goddess moves toward you with the two swords.

"Get back to your lesson."

You hold up your throbbing hand. "But my hand—"

She cuts you off before you can take that thought any further. "You must be able to find mental balance despite your pain. You need to overcome your emotions and your body. You must align to the energy of the swords."

You have no idea how you are going to do this; the pain is not just in your hand and arm, your mind has a firm grip on the pain as well. The goddess rips some silk from the bottom of her skirt and starts wrapping your wound.

"Healing can only happen when you no longer focus on the pain. See the healing, find the balance, and you will have mastered the swords."

She ties off the end of the silk and places one of the swords into your wounded hand. "Find the center and you will rest in a way you have never rested before."

You wince as you grab the hilt of the sword in your wrapped hand. Bending, you pick up the second sword and firmly grasp it in your healed hand. You raise them up just as you did before and the goddess once again blindfolds you. You falter the first couple of times, but eventually you are able to keep them in place. "Find the healing, find the center, find balance." The goddess's words echo in your ears as you reach desperately for something, anything not connected to the pain you feel. You search your mind, memories, and body for the thinnest of threads to another time and another place. Just when you think this entire exercise is pointless, you find it: the end of a thread. You pull on it with your mind and focus on where it leads. You feel a wave of relief start to wash over you as the thread becomes a scene.

That scene is one of your fondest memories. You focus with everything in you and make this scene come to life, full of sound, color, and smells. Relief gives way to a feeling of peace, and the feeling of peace morphs into joy, and suddenly your whole body feels light as a feather. Now *this* feeling you could stay in forever. It is the most relaxed—no, free—you think you have ever felt. And just like that, your awareness shifts and you drop the swords. You look at the goddess in confusion. She only grins down at you and pats the top of your head.

"Very good. Now you can rest."

Devotional Exercise

The Two of Swords asks you to decide, to make a decision and then to find balance and harmony with your choice. The Three of Swords teaches you how to stick with that decision even when things aren't going your way. The world is full of pain and suffering, and it will test your resolve and your mental strength. It won't be easy and you will falter. But part of knowing your strength is knowing that you can always come back to center and find your balance again no matter what is happening around you. As a Tarot Priestess, this won't mean that you will lack compassion or kindness—it just means you will be able to trust that you will always make the right call when your mind is focused on the result and not the problem. When we have this level of trust, we can slip into the Four of Swords easily, as we know the universe has our back and is doing its part to assist with the result we decided upon.

This is all part of learning to honor your decisions. Decision-making can very much be a devotional practice if you choose for it to be. You can even set up an altar for any decision you make and honor the goddess by lighting a candle once a day and sitting in meditation. During your meditation, see your end result and know that this is where your focus needs to be in order for you to remain balanced and light. If you are feeling the heaviness of the swords, you know your mind is not where it needs to be. Use your meditation time with the goddess to bring your mind and your swords back to center. Place items on your decision altar that represent your end result. Made a decision to relocate? Set your altar up to represent your new life in your new city, town, or country. Write a letter from your future self about all the fabulous things you have experienced since your move. You could even have a vision or mood board on it so you have something to focus on and steady yourself each time you come to the meditation cushion.

And of course, don't forget your tarot cards. Remove the Two, Three, and Four of Swords and place them where you can see them so you know the stages you are moving through. Just remember that altar spaces are deeply personal, so how you set up this altar is entirely up to you. This simple act of setting up an altar for your decision will help you through your Three of Swords moments, because they will come and will allow you to slip into the trusting state of the Four of Swords more easily. Sometimes the best action is no action except simple, quiet, still, meditation.

Bound, Unbound, and Healing the Wounds: Five, Six, and Seven of Swords

Now that you have rested and the goddess has fed and hydrated you, she moves you to another part of the valley. Here there are fallen trees all over the place. She walks over to one in particular that looks like a seesaw. She gestures for you to follow her and points to the middle of the log.

"Climb up there and stand still."

You do as she instructs and then watch as she plunges two swords into each end of the log. Then the goddess takes one more sword and passes it to you.

"This sword is your present. The swords at this end of the log are your future, and the swords at the other end are your past. Every time your mind brings up a thought, it is ruled by one of these three points in time."

You look left and then you look right—and suddenly realize your balance game just upgraded to a whole new level.

"Every time you allow your mind to weigh too heavily at either end of the log, you will be distracted from the sword you have in your hands. If this happens, you could do yourself harm. Your job is to stay centered, present in the moment. This time, keep your eyes open."

The goddess gives you that grin of hers and suddenly you feel uneasy about what sounds like a pretty simple task. You plant your feet in the middle of the log and start to balance yourself and the sword. Suddenly, you notice yourself leaning very heavily to the side of the future and the once weighty log under your feet is as light as a feather.

"Empty your mind," the goddess says from somewhere behind you. "You think you have already won, but you haven't even yet begun."

You center yourself once again and this time just start to focus on your breath. You concentrate as hard as you can on your inhale and exhale, keeping the focus on your breath, the feeling of your chest rising and falling, the breath making its way into your body. In and out. In and out. As you breathe, you notice you have finally started to even out again. And just like that, the log dips to the past and you find yourself imbalanced once again.

"Empty your mind, stay in the moment."

You grumble and adjust your weight once again. This time, you close your eyes to try and center yourself.

"Open your eyes. You must keep your eyes open."

You grumble again, but instead of resisting you find a spot on a tree in front of you. You notice the patterns on its bark and start to trace it with your eyes while breathing and staying focused. The more you look at the tree, the more you notice movement on the bark. Ants and other insects make their way in and around the tree. They seem extremely busy, and you simply watch them as you breathe. A light breeze rolls through the valley, making the leaves on the tree dance; you watch as they catch the sun through their movement. The scent of the valley fills each breath as you keep your attention on the tree. A bird makes its way down to the path of insects and starts to peck at them—all you want to do is shoo the bird away and tell it to leave the insects alone. At that moment, you feel it—you start to slip back down into the past as you feel more and more off-balance. As you slip, the goddess sticks another sword in the end of the log; you now have three behind you, two in front of you, and one in your hands.

"Focus. Clear your mind. Stay here."

Grumbling, you find your balance yet again as you hear a swan in the water beyond. You focus your mind on the water, imagining your log is a boat sailing out on the water. You imagine the spray of the water on your face and the slight breeze as it lets the scent of the lake up to your nose. You suddenly realize you have no idea how big the lake is. Where would you end up if you did try to sail across its surface? As your mind starts to seek, search, and figure out, you feel yourself off-balance yet again. You curse as you know that you have tipped into the future.

"Your thoughts are like robbers," the goddess says as she slams another sword into the future end of the log.

Now you have three swords behind you, three swords ahead of you, and one in your hand.

"Remember that when your mind strays too far ahead, it robs you of the gifts in the moment. When your mind drifts to the past, it steals the gift of the present. Stay here," she says as she points to the place between your feet.

Grumbling, you stand up as tall as you can. Instead of holding the sword, this time you plunge its tip in the spot the goddess pointed to. She laughs as you grunt with the force needed to keep the sword sticking upright in the wood.

"Yes! You've got it. Come, get down from your log."

"That's it?" you ask skeptically.

"Come," the goddess beckons as she continues to laugh. You are starting to think she is not done with you yet.

Devotional Exercise

The Five, Six, and Seven of Swords are interesting cards to look at as a story—these cards show you that in order to win, you have to leave something behind. In other words, there is always going to be a cost to forward motion. Sometimes we are fine to pay the mental toll, and at other times, we feel we are being ripped off or taken advantage of. The Five of Swords often shows how victory for one means pain and suffering for another. But it doesn't have to be. We could instead see this card as the card that tells us, "Your beliefs, thoughts, and ideas won't appeal to or win over everyone." The priestess path teaches us that we are not here to please other people. You may be here to be of service, but that does not mean you have to dim to fit in. This brings us to the Six of Swords, where you have to leave, remove yourself, or take a journey to resolve the issues that came up in the Five of Swords. In the Temple of Swords, this card represents the death of your guilt, the descent of the self to release guilt or even blame. You take these feelings into the underworld and leave them there. Which brings us to the Seven of Swords, which is the reminder to only take from the underworld that which you need. You don't need all of those swords. Some of them are meant to stay in the underworld. They were part of the descent. Do not grasp at them; let them slip from your fingers and fall to the floor. This sets up a beautiful spread.

CARD ONE: How is guilt for the victories of my life showing up?

CARD TWO: What is the best way to give this guilt to the underworld as a gift of devotion?

CARD THREE: What do I need to take with me from the underworld?

Once you have pulled the cards for this spread you can place them on your altar along with a picture of goddess Saraswati. You can also light a candle and recite your ode to the goddess from the beginning of this chapter.

Gifts of the Scar: Eight and Nine of Swords

The goddess leads you to what appears to be a stone maze whose entrance is hidden by overgrown trees, some of which look sharp and unfriendly. You stand quietly at the mouth of the entrance and wonder what on earth any of this has to do with your journey to the Temple of Swords. You watch as the goddess ties the seven swords from your training into a bundle. She motions for you to turn around and begins to strap them to your back. You keep waiting for your body to feel the weight of the swords on your spine, as you know from working with them just how heavy only one of them can be ... yet you feel nothing, as if all the goddess placed upon you is a ribbon of fabric. You even jiggle around to see if you can feel them shift or move on your back, but still nothing. You half expect the goddess to start laughing at you for not understanding what sort of magic she has cast upon the swords, but she does not. Instead as you turn to face her she looks very serious.

"This maze represents your ego mind. There are two more swords for you to collect and add to your pack. Once you have located them, the maze will show you the way out. The longer you stay in the maze, the more your mind will play tricks on you. So move quickly and don't allow yourself to get distracted or caught up in anything you may hear inside the maze."

Before you have a chance to ask any questions, she blindfolds you and pushes you from behind. You hear something close behind you, like a door sliding into place. The temperature drops and you now find yourself alone inside the maze. You walk straight ahead (the only direction you can) until you are forced to turn right. You only know this as you keep your hands on the side of the maze walls. As you round the corner, you hit something with your foot. You bend down and feel the coolness of metal seeping into your fingertips. You know this is your eighth sword. Carefully you find the hilt and pick it up. Just like the swords that are strapped to your back, this one feels weightless. You keep this sword out in front of you, moving it around like a cane to find your way through the rest of the maze.

The temperature changes suddenly as you feel the moisture in the air increase rapidly. Sweat beads under the blind fold and starts to drip down your face. Your eyes become wet and you can't concentrate on the maze anymore. Your body is struggling, and you could swear the sword in your hand just got as heavy as a boulder. Sweat makes your hands slip on the hilt of the sword and you drop it. As you crouch down to find the sword, you cut your finger on its blade. The pain of the cut mixed with the oppressive conditions in the maze are starting to make you anxious. Your heart rate speeds up, your breathing is shallow, and you feel like you are about to have a panic attack. You put your head between your knees and try to calm your breathing.

Suddenly, it occurs to you that you can remove your blindfold—the goddess never said you have to keep it on. You reach up to find the knot on the back of the blindfold only to find there was never one there. You pull it off and give your eyes a minute to focus. As you do, your body starts to calm down. Your heart rate slows and the air around cools once again. You tie the blindfold around your bleeding finger, pick up the sword, and start making your way through the maze. As you round what feels like the hundredth left corner, you see the last and ninth sword sticking out of the ground—and behind it is the exit. The only problem is that you have just walked into your worst possible nightmare: in order to retrieve the sword and leave the maze, you will either have to overcome it or get through it; staying where you are is not an option.

Devotional Exercise

As you move deeper through the lessons of the Temple of Swords, you will begin to see a pattern: the way your mind works, where it tends to wander, and how quickly you are able to correct it when it strays into territory you don't wish to dwell in. Here in the Eight and Nine of Swords, you have some healing work to do. You need to release those wounds and scars and let them go once and for all. This often happens when you can move from a logical mind to an inspired or divine mind. This is one of the ways the Eight of Swords works as it pushes you out of your comfort zone and makes you problem-solve in a new way. How well you adapt to this change and healing will show up in the Nine of Swords, as not everyone will experience this card with the same intensity.

If you have managed to allow this new way of thinking or problem-solving into your mind without too much resistance, then what you experience in the Nine of Swords will be more of an annoyance than anything else. However, if you doubt yourself and your abilities to get it right in the Eight of Swords, you may be suffering at the hands of the Nine of Swords. These cards offer you healing via examining your old mental scars. If your resistance here was not severe, you will be more willing to leave the old mental habits, beliefs, and nagging thought patterns behind you. But if you really struggled to let the divine or inspired mind in and your ego is screaming inside of your head, moving into the next phase of release is going to require deeper healing.

Pick up your journal and remove the Eight and Nine of Swords from your deck. Place both cards in front of you. Take a few slow, deep breaths and place your hands in prayer position, holding them at your heart. Call goddess Saraswati into your energy and ask her for healing around these two cards. You can stay in prayer pose and focus on the breath work for as long as you feel necessary, or you can pick up your pen and do some automatic writing with the goddess. Consider using the prompts below to get you started and in the flow of her energy. If you feel so inclined, you can turn over a card for each question and create a four-card spread. These cards might open up your communication with the goddess even more and allow you to explore these questions at a deeper level.

PROMPT/CARD ONE: Where is my resistance coming from?

PROMPT/CARD TWO: How can I learn to trust in my divine mind more deeply?

PROMPT/CARD THREE: Why is it important to heal this part of my mind?

PROMPT/CARD FOUR: Which beliefs or mental habits are causing me the most suffering?

Once you are done and feel you have gotten all the information you can, place your hands in prayer formation once more and thank the goddess for spending time with you. Take a few slow deep breaths as you give thanks and close out your session.

Leaving the Circle and Moving On: Ten of Swords

Battered and bruised, you step over the threshold of the exit from the maze. Your legs are so shaky that you know your knees can no longer support you. Exhaustion washes over your entire body and you collapse at the foot of the awaiting goddess. You can feel the full weight of the seven swords as they press into your back, causing pressure to build around your chest and lungs. You bring your focus to your breath, making sure you are breathing slowly and deeply. Now facedown in the dirt, you wonder if it might be easier to stay down, to just lie here and let the weight of the swords hold you down forever. Maybe your body won't hurt as much if you remain here—only pain seems to make its way to your mind when you try to move. Staying facedown in the dirt forever seems like a strange thing to be thinking about, but each sword pressing into your back and holding you down represents aspects of your life. They are those aspects that right now seem to be insurmountable, immovable, and hard. You aren't sure you have the strength to get up and deal with what needs to change, heal, and transform.

The goddess, however, has other ideas. She lifts the swords from your back and pulls you to your knees. She bends down and picks up the two other swords you dropped as you left the maze. The goddess walks you over to a circle made of stones. In the middle is a beautiful tree with a sword wrapped to its trunk. Leaves from the tree offer a healing canopy. You feel safe here, as if you could let this pain and exhaustion go once and for all. The goddess moves into the circle to offer the swords to the tree. As she places them into the ground around the trunk, the tree instantly grows around them. She looks over her shoulder at you to see if you are feeling up to putting the last and tenth sword into the earth, giving the final offering to the tree of wisdom. Even though you aren't exactly sure your legs can carry you, you make your way to the goddess with your arm outstretched and your hand open, ready and willing to receive the last sword. You feel its weight one last time and then plunge it into the earth. You take a step back as the ground beneath you starts to shift and shake as the tree's trunk expands to absorb your last piece of mental pain.

"You are complete now. Your time here has come to an end," the goddess says in almost a whisper. "You have done well, but now it is time to let this cycle end and to be done with all that has brought you to this moment."

You are so tired; all you want to do is lie down. But you are getting the feeling that the goddess won't be letting you rest here. She walks towards you and gently places her palm flat against your forehead.

"Close your eyes," she whispers, "and breathe."

You do as she says one last time. When you open your eyes, she is gone and you feel completely and fully restored.

Devotional Exercise

This is an ending, not just of your journey through the suit of swords but also of something you have carried with you in your mind. Whether it was a belief, a dream, a wish, a thought, or an idea, it has come to completion. It is now time to put it to rest once and for all; you have finished your journey with it. You have reached the end of the path as well as your time here. Remove the Ten of Swords from your deck and place it upon your Saraswati altar. Find a black candle if you can (if not, a regular tea light will be just fine) and get your journal and a pen. Light your candle and open your journal. At the top of the page, write: "This has now come to an end ... " Write underneath it, just letting the words flow. Try your best not to engage with your thinking mind—just let things bubble up to the surface of you head, down your arm, through the pen, and out onto the page. Don't try to make sense of what you are doing or even stop to think about what you are writing; just let it out.

When you feel like you cannot write anymore, pick up your cards and do this closing three-card spread:

CARD ONE: Why is this completion important?

CARD TWO: How can I best honor this ending?

CARD THREE: What is my next step?

You can write these questions and your answers to them in your journal so you can explore the messages in more depth. You can also add these cards to your altar and use them as part of your closing ceremony to the goddess. While your candle is still burning, say the following closing prayer to Saraswati:

Thank you, Goddess, for the gift

The lesson of swords

With a reset mind

I venture forth

To new adventures

I honor you, Goddess

Your compassion and patience

Blessed unto me

I give to you, dear Goddess

My humble servitude

Unfolding gratitude

Boundless love

May our connection remain strong

As this circle comes to completion.

We are one

Hand in hand

Heart to heart

It is done

Complete and whole

So it is.

Once your prayer and meditation time is up, blow out the candle to symbolize your time in the Temple of Swords, now at its end.

Chapter Seven

The Temple of Wands

Lighting Your World on Fire:
Priestessing with Lilith

———————————— ☽ ☽ ● ☾ ☾ ————————————

Ode to Lilith

Within the desert she does wander

Brimming with desire

Filled with wonder

Between the shadows

Beaming with light

The dark goddess does ignite

Brightly does she burn

Against the night

Fire dancing

Power in flight

She calls you forth

From pain and sorrow

To stand up tall

Head held high

To reclaim your might

Battle born you cry

Scarred and torn from the world outside

The goddess calls

Beckons you to come inside

Here in her halls you will be forged anew

The force of light

The Divine-made

Spread your arms

Tilt your head

Raise your voice and call her name

Lilith

Goddess

I come to thee

Awaken and restore me.

Kindle my fire

So all will see

They have not dimmed me

Introduction to the Temple of Wands

Welcome to the Temple of Wands, the domain of the fire goddess Lilith. Here you will learn what it means to live life with passion, desire, and spunk. The goddess will teach you how to light your inner fire, as well as how to feed it and fan its flames.

In this temple, you will focus on radiance, energy, and action. There is nothing passive about the teachings in this temple—lessons will come at you fast, and you could get burned if you are not careful. Goddess Lilith will teach you to connect to your fire and your deepest desires and fill you with passion and purpose. You will learn that there is no reason to be shy or timid in this material world. That all of it came to be because of the fire of creation. She will show you how your desire is holy, powerful, and the most spiritual aspect of your being. She will teach you how to practice devotion to all that lights you up. And she will instruct you on how to command, lead, and walk the world as if you too are a goddess and queen.

This temple is not for the faint of heart or the timid. Here is where you must step up and claim your power. Take your seat at the table of life and demand your share of the bounty. In the Temple of Wands, one does not ask for permission or seek acceptance. Instead, we move the force and power of holy fire. Come, step over the threshold. Ignite all that lies dormant inside you and allow the goddess to show you just how interesting this ride of life can be.

The Invitation: Accepting the Gift of Fire–Ace of Wands

They say the light burns the brightest in the dark, as the lack of light only showcases the splendor of the flickering flame. This is the beauty of contrast: the need for both the light and the dark, complementary spaces in which one can be free to explore all aspects of who they are and what talents they may have. Lilith knows this space well. She lives in the contrast, claiming all of herself, loving all of herself. She allows all of herself to be strong, capable, and resilient. There is power in owning the contrast of who you are. There is pleasure in seeing yourself as complete and whole. For it is only when you can be with all parts of yourself that you can embrace your purpose, your soul calling: the very reason you chose to step forward and wear the suit of the human experience.

Lilith beckons you closer toward the flames she tends, to stand before the light that is your soul and watch as the parts of it that can only be seen in the dark dance and move.

"Come closer, child of ash. Do not be afraid of your raw power. Step closer and see what burns inside of you," Lilith commands from her place near the forge.

The closer you get to the flames, the more the heat grows. You can feel your cheeks flush as the warmth starts to spread through your body. The closer you get to the flames, the more they seem to grow. It is as if the fire senses you or knows you.

"Move closer, it will not hurt you. Do not fear the aspects of yourself that have the ability to change your world forever. Let go of the stories you have been told about yourself and claim your heart's desire." Lilith moves her hands in and out of the fire as if to illustrate that the flames are harmless.

You take a few more steps and feel the sweat start to gather under your armpits and across your forehead. As you take a step, a small single flame jumps from the larger fire to dance right in front of your face.

"Hold out your hand, child of flesh and bone. Let it come to you."

You do as the goddess instructs and the flame jumps onto your palm. Although you can feel the heat radiating from it, it does not burn you. You study the flame as you notice it appears to have something inside of it. On closer inspection, you can see it is a movie of you dancing, looking completely free, lost in a moment of sheer joy. You smile as you allow the memories of this time in your life to flow to the forefront of your mind.

"Place the flame into your heart, child. Let it become one with you. Be the light you were always meant to be." Lilith moves her hand to her heart as if to show you what to do. You follow her instructions and feel this single flame as it merges with your body. It sends waves of electrified energy through you, like a jolt of awakening. When this happens, you see it all. It is as if you have the sight of the goddess for the very first time. You can see yourself as complete, whole, and powerful, the divine spark that you are. And just as quickly as it came, the sensation leaves you.

"Well done, child. Your journey back to the light has begun."

Devotional Exercise

We are born with light inside of us—it is the flame of life. It goes out when we leave this physical incarnation, leaving us to dissolve into ashes. Our life flame needs to be fed and tended to, which makes us all temple keepers to our inner flames, in essence. But how many of us have been taught how to honor, maintain, and grow what is inside of us? Learning to attend to the inner temple is a staple in all priestess lineages, and the Tarot Priestess path is no different. Your inner temple requires awareness, patience, and daily care. Lucky for you, Lilith is here to assist you in keeping your inner temple flame going.

The Ace of Wands is a fabulous card to work with when you need a reminder to attend to your inner flame. It is the torch of the soul, a reminder that light starts within you and that the light growing in you will illuminate the world outside your inner temple. In order for that light to grow, you need to know how to feed it and keep its flame vibrant and strong because many things in the outside world can dampen or dim your light. To check in on your flame and see how your inner temple would like you to tend to it, start by pulling the Ace of Wands card from your deck. Place it in front of you, picture side up. Pick up the rest of your deck and give it a shuffle. Hold the deck to your heart and imagine your life's fire surrounding the cards. See it dancing over them and tickling the deck. Once you feel your cards are fire-infused, cut your deck in half and take the top card on the bottom pile. Flip it over and place it next to your Ace of Wands. This is your daily message from the goddess, or how Lilith would like you to tend to your inner temple flame today. You can place these cards on your altar and light a candle, showing the physical act of tending to a flame. Meditate with the flame and your cards and see what other information the goddess has for you. Or you can take them to your journal and write on the message and meaning of the cards. You might wish to pick up your favorite tarot books or check the guidebook of the deck you are using. This exercise doesn't have to be long—it can be a very quick ten minutes. Practice it daily while you sit in the energy of the Temple of Wands.

Stepping into the Circle: Boundaries and Holding Sacred Space–Two, Three, and Four of Wands

When you are standing as one with the flame of the Divine, you feel powerful, strong, and capable of taking on the world. The goddess says this is how you felt before you returned to a physical body. The confident current of the Divine is you; you are one and the same as the vibration that holds all of your matter in place and allows you to be seen as whole, flesh and bone. The truth is that you are ash and dust, particles of star energy that have burnt out in order to rise and let you take your place on the stage of humanity. Here in the Two of Wands, you start to feel that connection to your power as if for the first time. You feel the energy pulse through you and are reminded of what your mind was originally created to do: create worlds. More specifically, you want to create a world you wish to live in and have dominion over. It is why you move from the Two to the Three to the Four of Wands: the cards of foundation, home, and belonging.

The space of your home, your body, your consciousness, the sovereign state that is you, is the sacred space Lilith wants you to be keeper of. You *are* the world you will relearn to make here in the Two and Three of Wands. Lilith will ignite your imagination; spark your curiosity about what is possible; and will show you how to clear the path to your wants, desires, and needs. She understands what burns inside you—a world trying to be born, screaming to be let out. Only you can guide it safely into the world of the senses. It is not enough to imagine what you want—you also have to feel it, see it, and hold its vibrational energy long enough for it to take form. All this fire energy starts to get a little tricky: you need to learn how to tend to your fire, feed it, nurture it, and make sure it doesn't burn yourself or anyone else. Wants, desires, and needs have an intensity to them, and sometimes it can all get out of hand. Thankfully you have Lilith to guide and show you how to use your power to create without harm.

The goddess moves toward you and gently holds your hands, turning them palms-up. She runs her finger down the middle of your hand. As she does so, you feel heat rise to the surface.

"Feel the energy in the palms of your hands. Focus on it. Maintain your concentration so the energy doesn't grow too fast," she says.

The heat in your hands increases, and it takes all of your concentration to keep your arms up and palms facing the heavens.

"Use your breath as a way to control the energy, to control the intensity of the desire that runs through your veins. The more control you have over your breathing, the more control over your ability to create. Loosen your focus and what you have built will go up in flames."

You close your eyes so you can't be distracted from the task at hand. As you do so, you feel the top of your head start to heat up as if to form a triangle of energy from both palms to your crown. You try your best not to let your concentration slip and focus on the world you want to create for yourself. What is it you truly desire to experience? If you really do hold the power in your own hands, how will you use it to better yourself and, in turn, those around you? These questions are not easily answered but more points of meditation. You let yourself slip into a deeper state of focus, allowing your ego mind to slip away so you can be more conscious of the universal energy that is pumping through you. The deeper you sink into this meditative state, the more heat begins to radiate from your chest, lighting up four points in your body: your palms, crown, and now your heart. You have become the four wands, the place of home inside yourself.

"Stay focused. You're almost there," the goddess whispers into your ear.

You know that your current state of this point of meditation is not something you can hold for much longer, but you do your best to peer even deeper into the void, into the darkness behind your eyes and beyond. There is a wild sense of losing yourself and finding yourself at the same time. As if becoming one with nothing, is becoming one with who you are. The heat in your body increases even more now; you feel like you are on fire, burning from the inside out. This energy, this power is inside of you, and it is so strong. How have you not felt it before? How have you gone this long without knowing that it resided in you all this time? And just like that it stops. A wave of cold damp air rushes over you.

"You shifted your mind. You moved it away from expansion and toward the lack. And with that shift, you lost your connection," the goddess explains as you open your eyes to see what happened. She continues: "We will practice again once you have given yourself time to rest. Do not worry, it is normal to wonder where this power came from and why you have not used it before. But if you keep holding the energy of lack, your power will become destructive. You were made to create and expand worlds, not destroy them with your regrets, anger, and fears."

Now it all makes sense: there was a piece of you that started to become resentful that you had this inside you the whole time but didn't know. The flick from excitement to anger was so quick and unconscious that you didn't even notice it. You were so lost in the questions that you weren't paying attention to the energy that arose with them. You raise your palms to your eyes but see no evidence of the heat that was just there. You rub at your chest and feel nothing that would indicate the energy that rose up from the heart, and just as cool to the touch is the top of your head.

"Do not worry, child of ash and earth. The power has not gone. It still lives in you, stronger than it was before. But now it is time to work on keeping your mind in the present and healing the past that made you question your abilities."

The goddess points to a chair near the fire; you walk over to it and take a seat. All of a sudden you become very weary, as if you have just walked a thousand miles and all you want to do is sleep.

Devotional Exercise

The following technique is one I wish I could take credit for, but alas I was not its inventor. Lucy Sheridan, my Comparison Coach, calls them "soul goals." I wish I could point readers to instructions or a talk she gave about it, but unfortunately I learned this while attending one of her online master classes. The process is not your ordinary goal-setting technique; it happens completely in your solar plexus, which just so happens to be your chakra center of fire. This technique is brilliantly aligned with the Two, Three, and Four of Wands, as it requires you to connect your soul fire and draw what your soul is seeking out of it. It is not an easy task, which is why I have modified it here as a spread. The difficulty stems from the ego mind. We all have beliefs around what is possible for us, and those beliefs live in our heads. But here in the Temple of Fire, under Lilith's loving watch, we aren't working with our heads—we are working with our gut.

For this exercise, remove the Two, Three, and Four of Wands from your deck and lay them faceup in front of you, starting with the Two and ending with the Four. Next, shuffle your cards and ask the goddess Lilith to come forward and infuse her energy into the deck as you hold your cards just above your belly button. Imagine Lilith's flames lighting up your deck of cards as smoke swirls through the cards. Take a deep breath and then draw your cards to match the spread below, placing the cards on top of the three in front of you.

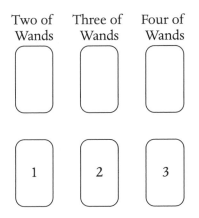

Two of Wands Three of Wands Four of Wands

1   2   3

CARD ONE: The spark of your soul goal

CARD TWO: How to build the energy of your soul goal

CARD THREE: How to prepare for your soul goal

A note about this spread: there are no good or bad cards here; there are merely cards that indicate how attuned you are with your soul goal. If you get cards that show you are a close vibrational match to your soul goals, it means you need to keep doing what you are currently doing. If you get cards that show you are not at all a match, it is time to do some healing work to get your head, heart, and body attuned to the new identity you wish to create. While doing this exercise, your soul goal may have planted a seed in your solar plexus, the energy center just above your navel. This seed wants to be nourished and it wants to grow, no matter what cards you ended up pulling. To connect even deeper with this energy, pull out your journal and do some free writing around your soul goal. Ask it questions and write whatever pops into your head as the answer. Opening this channel of communication with your soul goal will only strengthen your connection to it and help keep you on track with your thoughts, feelings, and actions. It's not always easy to let your inner flame lead, but the more you play, dance, and flow with your soul goal, the easier it will become.

Bound, Unbound, and Healing the Wounds: Five, Six, and Seven of Wands

Exhaustion is an interesting energy—it comes from both being depleted and also over-energized. The physical part of us needs to be trained slowly and gradually to hold energy. It can take months or even years for your physical vessel to attune to the vibrational frequencies of higher-level emotions. Emotions such as peace and love hold a high frequency and can change not just you but the energy around you too, including that of people who come into contact with you. For this reason, meditation, yoga, and ritual are life-long activities. It is only through discipline, repetition, and daily practice that the body learns to maintain the expansive energy required for peace, joy, and enlightenment.

Exhaustion happens on the way to awakening. It is part of the Tarot Priestess path. Yet, many experience it not in the way we are talking about now but in its lower-frequency state: anger, fear, doubt, jealousy. We all have an internal conflict inside of us and burn with conflicting emotions. Very few of us can consistently hold higher-frequency emotions all day long. The Five of

Wands is evidence that this is a universal phenomenon—we are not alone in our struggle. At the same time, this card also gives us a choice: We can stay in conflict or sort out our emotions, desires, and wants and aim them all in the same direction. Lilith asks you to make a choice here too. Will you allow yourself to be constantly exhausted by your lower base desires, or will you commit to the transformation she offers, stepping onto the path of the priestess to pledge your energy to the cause of peace, joy, and awakening? One of these choices will be an act of service, the other an act of suffering.

The Temple of Wands pushes us to burn off our old karma, to release all that no longer serves us and instead place it in the flames of Lilith's fire. In order to work the victorious path of the Six of Wands, you must shed your coat of suffering and struggle. Give yourself permission to shrug the weight of the past off your shoulders, and allow yourself to dream of what is possible in a world that you deliberately create from a place of love, compassion, and understanding. It is here you will learn that there are two types of desires: those which elevate you, and those which chain you to the wheel of eternal suffering. Lilith is here to assist you in making your choice.

She holds out her hand so that you can hold it tight when you feel uncertain or weak. She will stand by you when you slip and guide you back to the path. The work in the Temple of Wands will be crucial as you make your way through your Tarot Priestess training; you will need to take the role of Lilith in the lives of others. You will need to be able to see them, hold them, and guide them as they too step forward and join you on the journey to the higher frequencies of peace, joy, and abundance.

The first thing you must deal with is your own exhaustion; your weary self needs to create a better set of daily rituals. This will eliminate the constant struggle and allow you to focus all your energy in the same direction, which in turn will allow you to have success or at least a small victory in your life. The goddess also notices that when we are in constant conflict, we can't give ourselves the focus, attention, and energy needed to succeed at something. The size of the success is irrelevant in the eyes of the goddess; success energy holds the same frequency regardless of size. This is where the Six of Wands wants to bring you, to the vibration of success, to let you feel what it is like when you allow yourself to achieve something you desire. Here you can acknowledge that you created your victory and that it was perfectly okay to not only create but now celebrate it too. Lilith is not shy about celebrating her desires—she sees them as fuel for her soul. For this reason, she has no problem rallying support from her fellow priestesses. After all, people gravitate to the frequency of success. They all want to be a part of it. Humans instinctively feel the pull of the success frequency. This is evident in the next card Lilith wants to walk you through, the Seven of Wands.

The notion that humans are not islands is something that needs to be repeated over and over again until the idea is purged from humanity. Humans do better when they work together. Humanity is stronger when all come together to rally around a common cause. It is where true change and expansion come from. I see it in the mastermind groups I create for high-achieving entrepreneurs. Our clients do so well because we hold a vortex of community success. We amplify the energy as a group—not islands, but a mass of swirling victory. It is time to heal your island syndrome, the feeling that you need to be and do it all yourself, and say it's just easier if you deal with it by yourself. The vibration of success requires others in order for it to grow.

Ripples of strength and solidarity are cast into the energy of time and space when we celebrate our wins with others. Lilith wants you to understand that this is not a selfish act. As you move even further along the Tarot Priestess path, the more important it will be for you to continually point this out to others in your life. The more you celebrate the fulfillment of your desires, the more able you are to hold space for someone else to do the same. The Tarot Priestess knows that it all starts with them; what the priestess is capable of is fostered in all those around them. For this reason, Lilith wants you to take in deeply the lessons offered here in the Temple of Wands. Focus on your desires and harness their energies. Allow yourself to create something out of that energy, celebrate it, and allow others to rally to your side in honor of your achievements. This is not about ego—it is the bursting forth of the soul self in order to make the everyday human experience more joyful, exciting, and adventurous.

Devotional Exercise

Although the Five of Wands is not a mental card, it is the card I personally associate with what I like to call "squirrel brain," which is when you have so much to do but no idea where to start. Everything and everyone is competing for your attention and you just want to scream. I experienced this very phenomenon while editing this book. If you don't deal with your Five of Wands energy, it can quickly become a Tower moment. A Tarot Priestess is aware enough to know when they are in the energy of certain cards, so if you have been suffering from squirrel brain, I have a solution for you (and no, I did not invent it). The technique is called the morning pages, from the book *The*

Artist's Way. You don't have to do it in the morning, and what appears here is a modified version of the technique. Although it is basically a simple brain dumping exercise, it is incredibly powerful. For this exercise you will need your Five of Wands card facing up in a place where you can see it. You will also need a timer (either on your phone or a kitchen timer), a pen or pencil, and a journal or notepaper.

While the process is easy, it is not necessarily simple. (I have been doing it for five years now and sometimes I struggle to even get through it!) Set your timer for twenty minutes. Hit the start button and write. Keep writing until your timer runs out. You want to get as much of that noise out of your head onto that paper as you can. The more you write, the more space you will free up for any work you need to do. The more chatter you release, the more you can hear the inspired voice of the goddess. The very act of sitting still for twenty minutes and writing by hand will ground all that fire energy into the present moment. If you want to amplify the experience, put on your headphones and listen to some chants, solfeggio frequencies, classical music, or some other music that calms your nerves, slows your mind, and settles your soul. You may also be pleasantly surprised how much more vibrant you feel after you have let go of all that loud, heavy noise that was weighing you down.

Once your timer goes off, stay in your chair and move on to your Six of Wands task, which is to write down three wins you had from the previous day. It could be anything—size isn't the point here. You just want to feed your success vortex now that your energy is nice and grounded and focused. Personally, I often claim putting on real pants as a win. I work from home and don't always need real pants, so putting them on feels like a victory. I might also write down having a peaceful day as a win, or even not face-planting into cake. I think you get the idea. Just make sure you do this right after you finish your twenty-minute free-writing brain dump. After that, you are going to move into the energy of the Seven of Wands and share one of your wins with either a friend, a group you belong to, or even a family member and celebrate together. We have our students and clients post their wins every week in our Facebook group. The act of doing so creates a sacred space with the energy of the Seven of Wands in real time. We amplify the victory in a group while giving energetic support to their success vortex—some good Tarot Priestess work right there!

If you want to take all this one step further and really get into your Tarot Priestess role, you might even use these cards in a spread for someone else and guide them in the exercises above. Try this simple three-card spread:

CARD ONE: What is causing your Five of Wands squir-rel brain?

CARD TWO: What win or victory do you need to honor and celebrate?

CARD THREE: Who would support you best in cele-brating your wins?

Gifts of the Scar: Eight and Nine of Wands

The goddess hands you a lit wand burning with her special fire and asks you to light the remaining seven down the cave path to the opening below. This is the act of lightbearer and wandering illumination. Where you go, so does the light. Wherever the light goes, it creates a path and draws others to it.

"You illuminate the path by lighting one wand at a time," the goddess speaks from beside you. "The light works best when it is honored, one spark and one flame at a time. It is only then that you notice its gift and healing. So many ask to have all the light turned on instantly, not knowing it would only blind them, turning the blessing into a curse. This is why desire is repressed in your human world. It is no longer used to enlighten; instead, it is used to dull the senses and blind one to their true light."

You stop and let the goddess's words sink in. Is this why you have struggled and not allowed yourself to be open to desire? Have you have been afraid of being dulled, or even overtaken with a power you did not know how to control? Your feet find themselves moving and you keep walking along the path, lighting one wand at a time and reciting the mantra the goddess whispered in your ear before you began:

"My desire sees your desire, my light honors your light, together we shall be illuminated."

You continue slowly, making sure you feel each step along the path as you move between the wands. Every movement, word, and thought is intentional. For the first time in a really long time, you don't feel rushed, though there does seem to be a building intensity as you light each wand. You feel more purposeful. As the path lights up, your body feels like it is humming, a physical sensation slowly building inside of you. You are more attuned to the path, as if you and the fire are vibrating at the same frequency. It is funny how you have never really noticed the difference between intensity and speed; they feel so much alike, yet have subtle differences that you now feel running through your body. This feeling lets you know that perhaps you have misidentified these feelings in the past and they might have caused you to act in a way that was not entirely suitable. It may have even brought about a less-than-satisfying end result. But with the goddess by your side guiding you, slowing you down, and making sure you stay in beat to the fire, you feel the energy build. Something has awakened inside you, and you know without a shadow of a doubt it won't be extinguished anytime soon.

As you move closer to the end of the path, you become incredibly aware of the light that now surrounds you—the whole path is aglow, and it looks like you are walking through a tunnel of gold. There is a luxurious feeling to this experience, so much so that you slow your pace even more to soak up as much as possible. You want to imprint all the sensory experiences of this moment upon your mind and heart. You want to remember what it feels like to be seen, to be expressive and illuminated. If this is what true desire feels like, you want to make sure you feel it in every cell of your body so you can replicate it again and again and again. As if by instinct, you take a mental snapshot of this moment, wrapping it in a sensory blanket before storing it away for later recall.

You come to the end of the path. Seven illuminated wands bathe the area in golden light. One wand still blazes in your hand and you see another at the end of the cave next to the goddess. You know that once you step beyond where she is, this experience will be over. The weight of that understanding almost brings you to your knees.

"Come, child of ash. Your time here is coming to an end, and we have one more lesson to discuss before you leave this temple and move on."

You look back over your shoulder and misplace your footing, causing you to land face-first in the dirt at the goddess's feet.

Devotional Exercise

The Eight of Wands is an intense card; I often feel as though I am under attack when I see those eight wands flying out of the image. That is not the energy this card carries with it, however—this is the card of the clear path, the one that is open and ready for you to walk. As a Tarot Priestess, you will know this path due to the light it radiates. It will have a glow to it that lets you know that the goddess herself has opened a way for you. This light may light the way to a solution, the path to a new partner, or even the removal of a block in front of your success. Just know that when this card walks into your readings, it is saying that something you desire has the welcome light on.

The Nine of Wands is the "you made it" card. Despite all the obstacles in your way, you made it through to the other side of the Eight of Wands. The Tarot Priestess experiences this card in a way that honors all the trips, falls, and missteps that led them to this point. Life is not a perfect journey. Going for what your heart desires isn't easy. You will stumble, trip, and fall along the way. But you were able to dust yourself off and see it through to the end. The goddess sees all that you have been through but wants you to know that the only thing that matters is where you are now. Looking back is pointless. Everything that you have been through has changed you. You look at yourself and the world in a new light.

For this exercise, pull your Eight and Nine of Wands cards out of your deck. Place them faceup in front of you. Starting with the Eight of Wands, place your hand on the card and take a few deep breaths. If you feel inclined, you can close your eyes here to allow yourself to focus deeper. As you connect with this card and focus your breath, allow the energy of the card to show you where the path of illumination has opened in your life. You might see flashes of images or hear words—just go with the information in whatever form it appears. Keep breathing and maintain the connection to the card for as long as you can. Once you feel the connection has broken, you can record your findings in your journey. This is a form of channeling, allowing the card to speak directly to you. If you did not get anything the first time, you can try again. If you need extra assistance, pick up your deck, give the cards a shuffle, and flip over the top card. Place it next to the Eight of Wands and see what the cards have to tell you.

When you know which area of your life has been illuminated and you have a stronger sense of why now is the time for this block or path to be cleared, focus on your Nine of Wands card. Open your journal and write a small gratitude prayer for all the people, places, and situations that have bought you this illumination. You may even wish to journal about how you have changed for the better because of what you have overcome. Just let the words flow and see what comes up as you write your prayer. Once you have finished, pick up your deck and give it another shuffle. This time, you are going to see what happens now that you have made it. What is the message the goddess wants you to know? Again, flip over only the top card from the deck and place it next to your Nine of Wands.

If you want to take this exercise a step further, take all four of these cards and place them on your altar. Light a candle and say your prayer to Lilith out loud. This act of devotional ritual will ground the energy of this exercise, not to mention honor the teachings and lessons the goddess has bestowed upon you.

Leaving the Circle and Moving On: Ten of Wands

"What is done should not become a distraction. Stay focused on where you are going, not where you have been."

The goddess smirks as you brush the dust and dirt off yourself.

"Looking back is an act of suffering. Look instead at where your feet are now."

As you glance at your own feet, you suddenly realize something: The ground you stand on has changed. It is no longer the dusty floor of the cave. Instead it is a path, one you know. It is the same one you found at the very beginning of your journey to the temples.

The goddess reaches out her arms. "Give me the desires you no longer need, the ones which have been met. You do not need to keep holding them as if nothing better will ever come your way."

At first you are unsure what she is talking about until you see the pile of burned sticks at your feet. You bend to gather them and see there are ten. They feel heavier than they look; you bend your knees and bring them into your arms before handing them over to the goddess. As you extend your arms, she touches the bundle and they turn to butterflies and fly away.

"What has been fulfilled needs release so it can be transformed into something new. The more you hold on to it, the longer you deny it and yourself a new life. A burden is nothing more than an old memory you have carried for too long. Letting it go is how the energy of creation continues to be born again."

The feeling that comes over you now is the same one you have experienced at the end of the other journeys with the other goddesses. You know it has come to an end and that at any moment, Lilith will be gone. The goddess steps forward and places her hand upon your chest. You feel the warmth of her touch spread throughout your whole body.

"Remember who you are, child of dirt and mud, daughter of ash. The world lives within you. You are the spark, and only you will light your way."

The heat inside you rises as you feel the intensity of her statement awaken something deep inside you. Then, just as quickly, it is gone, and the goddess along with it. You once more find yourself at the very spot where you started this journey, at the beginning of the path.

Devotional Exercise

There comes a time when we must lay down the past, when the burden becomes too great and we need to lighten our load. The weight of the past smothers the spark of our inner fire and stops us from blazing with the desire of creation. Here at the end of your journey with the Temple of Wands, you can set that burden down; hand it over to the goddess and let it go. Allow it to be transformed into something new, and feel the freedom to do the same. Do this exercise the day before the new moon or as close to it as possible. Pull your Ten of Wands card from your deck and place it on your altar. On a piece of paper, write down all that you wish to let go. Let those heavy, weighty memories of the past that no longer have a place in your world leak onto the paper and out of your energy.

Once you feel you have written all you can, fold the paper in half and then in half again. Now rip it to shreds, tearing it up into as many pieces as possible. Place these pieces of paper in a small bowl and place that on your altar along with your Ten of Wands card. On top of your shredded paper, sprinkle some salt, dirt, and dried rosemary. The next items for your altar are a black candle and a white candle. Light the black candle first, letting it burn for a few minutes, then burn the white candle. The black candle is for releasing, letting go, and breaking the bond of the past. The white candle is to purify and clear the old energy. You can have these candles in separate holders or place them next to each other on a plate, dripping a little wax on the bottom of the candles to make them stick. Once your altar is set up and your candles are both burning, recite the following prayer:

> Lilith, I call to you
>
> Step forth and take from me
>
> All the burdens
>
> All the pain
>
> All the rage
>
> That I no longer need
>
> Feed me instead
>
> Nourish me
>
> Relight my flame
>
> Spark the desire
>
> The one that resides inside of me
>
> Clear my energy

Heal my heart

Take these ripped shreds

Recycle these items

And weave them back

Into threads of creation

From this moment something ends

Yet with your spark

I will begin again.

I am the light

I am the power

Goddess Lilith, I am desire

And so it is.

If it is safe to do so, leave your candles to burn all the way down. If you do not have a lot of time, consider using birthday candles, which burn very quickly. Once your candles have burned down, take any remaining wax and mix it into your paper shreds. Place everything in a paper tea bag or a very small canvas bag and bury it in your backyard. If you do not have a yard, throw it in the trash; your spell is contained and bound inside the bag.

Your time with the Temple of Wands is now over. You have moved through all its lessons, from Ace to Ten. You are free to come back and work on any lesson, card, or exercise you want at any time.

Chapter Eight

THE TEMPLE OF CUPS

**Healing with the Priestesses
of Avalon**

)) ● ((

Ode to the Lady of the Lake

From the water she rises

Dripping with all that was and could be

Staring into the now

Above her head a cup she holds

Rays of gold radiate

Glistening drops cascade down the sides

Answers you seek

Wishes fulfilled

Granted if you dare

She rises still

Moving gracefully towards the shore

Ripples casting future predictions

Fates of the unknown washing away

Yet still she rises

The cup overflows

Potential to spare

Priestess bow in her rising

Devotional everyday acts

Nature as ritual

Upon the shore she stands

Cup placed upon the land

Come be anointed

The invitation to initiation

All that you seek is within

Introduction to the Temple of Cups

Welcome to the Temple of Cups, the domain of the priestesses of Avalon. Here in this temple you will learn that the world is your mirror, that what you create inside you will be reflected in the world outside you. In this temple you will learn how to guard your emotions, still your raging waters, and create a world in which you can do more than just survive—you will learn how to thrive. The priestesses of Avalon will walk you through the temple and its cups. They will instruct you how to fill your cups, how to empty them, how to clean them, and what to do if they crack or break. In the Temple of Cups, you will take a journey to the emotional body. Through this emotional body you will be asked to confront your fears, be mindful of your attachments, and be careful of your fantasies. You will learn the difference between creating a dream and being stuck in one.

The priestesses of this temple will show you your reflection and make you study it completely and wholly, not allowing you to look away or turn your head from the truth of what you create and why you create it. This is the temple where you can be reborn. You can be cleansed, restored, and healed anew from the sacred water of the cups. Trust the flow of the lessons and be respectful of the priestesses. After all, you have entered their temple to master your emotional body, expand your life in ways that you have only ever dreamed of, and learn to control your creative force. Cross the threshold, pick up the cup, and take your first sip if you dare.

The Invitation: Accepting the Gift of Water— Ace of Cups

The overflowing cup from the Lady of the Lake stands on the shore. It looks to have grown five sizes, as if placing it upon the land has given it the power of the trees. Also known as the High Priestess of the order of Avalon, the Lady of the Lake beckons you forward. She wishes to bless you and anoint you with the holy water of her lake, water that holds the prayers of champions and legends in the making. The rest of the priestesses form a circle around you, the cup, and the Lady. They stand in meditative silence, holding the space, grounding the energy, and protecting your initiation. You feel openness and an honest sense of a group of people who only wish for you to feel a sense of belonging and wholeness. You move slowly toward the Lady and her oversized chalice, which you can now see is ornately engraved with images of dragons, knights, and magical scenes. Crystals have been added to the rim of the cup; when the light hits them, you see thousands of miniature rainbow light beams. The whole scene feels like a dream, yet still you walk.

The Lady stretches out her arm, signaling that she wishes you to join her. You step up next to her and take her hand. Her smile never wavers—it is firm, constant, and reassuring. She dips her fingers into the cup, speaking words in an old language you do not understand. With one hand still wrapped around yours, she takes the fingers of her other hand and places them on your heart, right in the middle of your chest, and blesses you. She again dips her fingers into the cup, never once stopping her chanting prayer. This time, she touches the middle of your forehead. Once more her fingertips find the water inside the cup and once again she blesses you, this time on the top of your head. She takes both of your hands in hers now, facing palms up as she moves you closer to the cup. She places the tips of her fingers on both hands into the water and flicks them onto your palms, drawing some sort of symbol into your skin. You can't see it as much as you can feel her fingers act like paintbrushes over your upturned hands.

When she is finished with the symbols, she closes your palms and places them in a prayer position next to your chest. She raises her hands over her head and all the other priestesses surrounding you do the same. Together they begin to chant, "Arise, sister of Avalon, rise!" This chant is repeated over and over for about a minute or two. When the chanting has stopped, your initiation is now complete. You have entered the Temple of Cups and have been accepted as one of the sisters. Your journey with the Lady is now ready to begin.

Devotional Exercise

Grab your tarot deck and remove the Ace of Cups card—it is time to see what blessings the priestesses of Avalon wish to bestow upon you. This is a very simple five-card spread with the Ace of Cups in the center as the significator. Place this card faceup in front of you, making room for the next four cards. Hold the rest of your deck up to your heart and take a slow, deep breath as you connect your cards to your heart. As you breathe, ask the Lady to show you what blessings she is flowing into your life today while remembering that there are no bad cards, only cards filled with love, healing, and solutions. Once you feel a connection between yourself, the cards, and the Lady, remove your cards from your heart and give them a shuffle. Pull four cards and place them around your Ace of Cups:

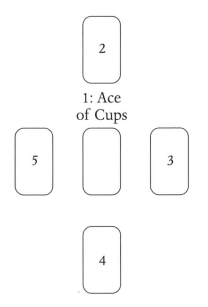

CARD TWO: How the Lady will bless you in health; this card shows how your health can be improved, maintained, or how you can shift how you feel about your overall health and well-being.

CARD THREE: How the Lady will bless you in love; this card shows how you can open up your heart more and receive more love. It could illustrate how your heart currently looks, how it is healing, or even how it likes to receive love.

CARD FOUR: How the Lady will bless you with wealth; this card shows how to let more wealth and prosperity into your life. It might mean learning how to feel into it, how to think yourself into it, or how to vibrationally move yourself into wealth's path. Sometimes the blessing is clarity or illumination on the way forward.

CARD FIVE: How the Lady will bless you spiritually; this card will give you an indicator of where your focus, prayer work, and meditation need to be. Oftentimes we get so caught up in the act of doing things that we forget that our spiritual practice has a very distinct purpose. Let the Lady bless you with the gift of purpose.

Once you have finished with your spread, you can take these cards and place them on your altar. Light a candle and give a small prayer of thanks to the Lady and your Avalonian sisters. Thank them for blessing you and showing you where you can move forward, expand, and be more open and receptive. Sit in meditation with this energy for a couple of minutes and just let yourself absorb your blessings. When you feel you have finished, blow out your candle and continue with the rest of your day/evening.

Stepping into the Circle: Boundaries and Holding Sacred Space–Two, Three, and Four of Cups

To take the next step on your journey inside the Temple of Cups, you will need to open your heart and allow it to lead the way. This temple is not guided by the head; the mind is not master inside this sacred space—instead, it is all about the feelings that flow straight from your heart out into the world around you. If this is the first time you have been asked to navigate with your heart, do not despair: the sisters are here to assist and guide you under the watchful eye of the High Priestess of Avalon. If, however, you are always following your heart, know that you will be asked to refine that skill in this temple. There is always room for improvement, and there are always more ways for your heart energy to expand and grow.

The sisters move toward you and ask you to follow them to what looks like a stone altar. On it you see four chalices filled with water. The Lady takes the first cup and pours the contents out over the altar as if to wash it clean. She then takes the second and third cups and ties a red ribbon around each of their stems. She passes one of the cups to you and she keeps the other. She tells you to drink. She holds your gaze as she lifts the cups to her own lips and you mirror her actions. She takes a deep drink from the cup before throwing the remaining contents onto the altar, telling you to do the same. The fourth and final cup she picks up along with the three empty cups and hands them off to one of the sisters who walks them to the lake's edge. The sister lays the three empty cups down in the mud and leaves the fourth one upright. She sits beside them, gazing off to the water beyond. You wonder what she is looking at, but your attention is brought back to the altar and the Lady. She wants you to focus on her and asks you to come closer. She places one hand on your heart and the other on her own chest.

"This is a true sacred circle, the loop from your heart to mine, the sharing of heartbeats. It must be protected, it must be revered," she says as she looks deep into your eyes. She begins to chant in a language you do not understand, yet the vibration feels like something you have heard before. The experience feels intimate but not in a sexual way; it is safe and familiar. In fact, you feel as though you have experienced all of this before, a ghost of a memory that you cannot quite form. You take a deep breath and think about the journey you have taken so far to get to this temple and the lessons you have already learned. You look deep into the Lady's eyes and let yourself get lost in them just for this moment, just right now.

Devotional Exercise

The space around your heart is sacred and should be treated as such. When you understand the importance of this space, you no longer allow it to suffer as you set up strong yet flexible boundaries around it. The Two and Three of Cups establish these boundaries. With these boundaries, you allow only those who share similar heartbeats into your inner circle and honor the messages your heart sends out into the world. The Two sets up the energy of heart-based partnerships. While usually platonic in nature, it has the potential to grow and blossom into something more. The Three of Cups extends this energy into larger social circles, bringing in more and more people whose heartbeats match the rhythm of your heart energy. Such people feel passionate about the same things you do, and they hold the same vision for the world. There is without a doubt a heart connection.

Remove your Two and Three of Cups from your deck and place them in front of you. These two cards work as a pair, so let's do a magical pair reading with both. Pick up the rest of your deck and hold it to your heart. Close your eyes and call in the energy of the Lady of the Lake, the High Priestess of Avalon. Feel her energy move into the cards and flow through your heart center. Take a few slow, deep breaths and then shuffle your cards. Draw one card and place it on top of the Two of Cups, then draw another card and place it on top of the Three of Cups. These cards show how you see your heart-based relationships. They give you a snapshot of how your heart communicates with those you consider close and those you deal with in the larger world. These cards will also show how you experience heart connections.

If you see any cards from the suit of swords, it is an indicator that you tend to intellectualize your feelings; the energy is very much cerebral. The suit of cups shows you are very sensitive and these sort of relationships are very important to you. Pentacles show you that you consider relationships to be work and that dealing with your feelings takes time. Wands show how quickly you like to burn through your feelings, passion that is intense and over almost as quickly as it began. If you wish to go deeper, spend some time with these cards in your journal.

To finish this exercise, remove the Four of Cups from your deck and place it on your Temple of Cups altar. This card is about the mundane, everyday maintenance of your heart-based relationships. Keeping the heart open and flowing is not easy, nor is it glamorous. Yet all priestesses know it is essential. This card represents your daily practice here in the temple of Avalon. For the duration of your time here, you will keep this card on your altar. Each morning you will light a candle and write a gratitude list of all the things you are grateful for when it comes to your heart-to-heart relationships. It doesn't have to be a long list, just a way of tapping into the everyday power and magic that is your sacred, divine, and resilient heart. Once you are done, blow your candle out. You may even consider buying a special pink candle just for this exercise. Follow the nudges of your Avalon sisters, who will always show you the way of your heart.

Bound, Unbound, and Healing the Wounds: Five, Six, and Seven of Cups

Loss and letting go can shrink or harden the heart, yet here in the Temple of Cups you are being asked to keep it open and to keep it soft. Gentle compassion is healing and keeps the flow of your waters pure. The High Priestess of Avalon knows loss well. She may have made many a legend, but she has also lost them; in her time, she has seen many become arrogant in their greatness and fallen to the underworld, never to shine in the light again. Falling and rising, rising and falling—it is all part of the same energy, the energy of the Five of Cups. One of the priestesses takes the fifth cup and places it upright next to the three cups lying in the mud by the shore of the lake and alongside the lone upright cup.

The Lady looks you deep in the eye and asks, "Which set of cups is your heart drawn to first? Those that have been spent or those standing ready to be filled?"

You understand at once this is not a question you answer out loud; it is intended for for meditation, something to ponder and be aware of, not just now but in the future as well.

"If you focus on what has been spent, you will find yourself stuck in loss. You will grieve for what was and not understand the potential the moment has. If you focus on the upright cups, you look to the future and allow yourself to dream." The Lady gestures to one of the priestesses, who places two more cups on the shore for a total of seven cups.

"Your heart will let you know where your mind is hooked. It will either be in the past and the suffering that looking back causes or in the future, dreaming of the potential just waiting to be tapped."

You nod your head; you understand her meaning completely. You may not wish to reveal your heart to the Lady just yet, but do not be fooled—she knows without you telling her. She can feel you. After all, your energy vibrates with every beat of your heart. There is no way she does not know what you feel and where you mind is.

"It is normal to acknowledge what has been lost … or in this case, spilled. We can see that the contents of the cup soak back into the earth and nourish the soil, mixing with the water of the lake. We rejoice in this merging of energies and allow ourselves to dream of what new life these waters can provide. It is not healthy, however, to keep the mind on the spill or try to replace that which is gone in the cup once more."

You nod again and notice that her metaphor is as large as life. There is a profound lesson in the Lady's words, yet it is simplistic in nature. However, you have learned over the years that simple does not equate to easy. It is one thing to know this lesson in theory, but it is another to take this teaching and embody it, live it, and use it as a daily practice.

Devotional Exercise

Healing from emotional wounds can be tricky, as it often requires us to bring pain back up in order to let it go. The Five of Cups offers you a gift in the healing process, asking you to focus on the gifts that were created in the pain's wake. The two upright cups are indicators that what you are letting go is a natural step in the process of your expansion. Two gifts are waiting for you to claim. They are right there—all you have to do is reach out and take them. Wherever your mind is focused dictates your next step. Here you get to choose and exert your free will, using your mind. You may not be in a place where you feel better just yet, but your mind can help you make a decision about how you want to proceed to get to that better place. The two choices on offer are staying in the past (the Six of Cups) or dreaming about a possible new future (the Seven of Cups).

The following spread gives you a window into how your heart and mind are aligned (or misaligned) when it comes to the healing gifts the the High Priestess of Avalon has bestowed upon you. First remove the Five, Six, and Seven of Cups from your deck and place them in front of you in a triangle, with the Five of Cups at the top.

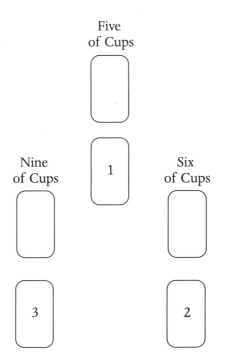

Five
of Cups

Nine
of Cups

1

Six
of Cups

3

2

Now pick up the rest of your deck and give it a shuffle as you focus on the triangle. Take a couple of slow, deep breaths. Hold the deck to your heart and close your eyes. Think about an emotional wound that you are ready to let go of once and for all. You know it's time to start the releasing process—the energy is toxic to your current experience. You feel that toxicity like an anchor weighing you down. When you are connected with this wound, select one card and place it on top of the Five of Cups. Shuffle your cards again and hold them next to your heart. Now think about how this wound is keeping you attached to the past. What cord needs to be cut right now in order for you to stop drifting to the past? If you need to, call in the energy of the Lady and her priestesses to surround, support, and protect you. Now select one card and place it on top of the Six of Cups. Shuffle your cards one last time and hold them once more against your heart as you take some slow, deep, steadying breaths. It is time to claim your gift. Your pain was not for nothing; you were birthing something miraculous, though you may not have been fully aware of it. When you feel ready to claim your gift, select your card and place it on top of the Seven of Cups. You will now have a three-card spread:

CARD ONE: The wound

CARD TWO: The cord

CARD THREE: Claiming the gift

The triangle of this spread is a portal for the Lady, who offers you healing energy through these cards. If you'd like, you can sit with these cards in this position and receive the healing. Close your eyes and allow yourself to receive the energy the priestesses of Avalon send your way. Their energy will move through your emotional body and assist your heart. If you didn't want to read the cards at all, this alone would still be powerful. You can also use this triangle for meditation. To go deeper and really explore the possibilities you have uncovered for expansion, break out your journal. Although powerful in and of itself, this spread is merely the first layer in a deeper healing, one that you can dive into through your sacred journal practice. Gather all your favorite tarot books and explore the meanings of the cards further, moving between intuitive writing and intentional research. How you work with this triangle is totally up to you. You may use one of the above suggestions or even do them all. It really depends on how deep and old the wound you are letting go of is.

Gifts of the Scar: Eight and Nine of Cups

"So what will it be, little one?" The Lady turns and faces the cups.

"The future," you answer. It is the only answer your heart will allow. You cannot go back in time or change what has already been. You can only be in the energy of what you are creating. One of the priestesses moves toward you with another cup filled with water and hands it to you.

"Take this cup into the lake. Pour out the pain in your heart and the wounds you have been keeping open. Then fill the cup with water from the lake and bring it to me."

You take the cup and wade into the water. The water is cool but not unpleasantly cold and has a silky feeling to it as it wraps around your calves. The bottom of the lake is soft like pillows, not at all how you imagined it. You go in as far as your knees and hold the cup to your heart. You imagine the hurt you have been carrying all this time flowing out of your heart and into the cup. You even give it a color and see colored light energy pour out of you and into the cup. The more you allow this energy to come out of you, the more you can feel the release. Your body tingles all over as you clean and clear these old wounds, being thankful for the lessons and blessing the points of expansion. There is no doubt in your mind that you would not be standing in a lake right now if it was not for the gifts of this pain—it shaped you and showed you who you really are. That pain served a purpose, and now it is time to let it go. The energy turns off like a tap, a physical sensation you feel in your body. You know it is time to pour the contents of the cup into the lake. You look for a spot that feels right and slowly begin to pour. As you do, the priestesses start chanting on the shore. You

close your eyes and allow the vibration of their chant to surround you, breathing it in like a healing balm.

Your cup is now empty; it is time to fill it up. But you do
not draw from the same place you just released your heart's
pain. You take your cup and walk away from the pain once and
for all. You find a place on the lake under a willow tree. The
light around it seems to glow and sparkle. This is where you
will draw the water for your future self. The priestesses are still
chanting but the sound has changed; it does not sound as som-
ber. You reach down into the water under the willow and fill
your cup. As you raise it out of the lake, you notice that the
water inside has the same sparkle and glow as the tree. It looks
magical. You carefully carry it back to the shore and hand it
back to the Lady, who takes the cup and splits the water into
one more cup.

"This cup represents the future you, the person you are
creating right here, right now. It is the you who is filled with
dreams for a life she is now beginning to live. This other cup
represents the world you wish to engage with. This is your wish
for the world outside, for people you may or may not meet.
One cup holds the compassionate possibility for yourself, the
other for the world."

She begins to pray over both cups and you feel her prayer.
You notice the air shift around you as if it is suddenly filled with
electric energy, sizzling with magic. You place your hand over
your heart and breathe deep. The words of the Lady's prayer
seem to seep into your skin and all the way to your bones. It
is as if she is creating you all over again, bringing into being a
you who was reborn from the lake. Tears form at the corners
of your eyes, but not from sorrow or joy—these tears are from
a deeper part of you, the you who is letting go, surrendering,

and being reborn. You let it all in and resist nothing. You are so lost in the moment that you have not noticed the Lady is finished with her prayer. It is not until one of the priestesses gently touches your shoulder and indicates it is time to eat that you move. You rub your eyes and gather yourself, knowing now that this part of the process is well and truly over. Take some more breaths to steady and ground yourself into the here and now. Once you feel you are safe to move your legs, you follow the priestess to the feasting area.

Devotional Exercise

One of the heart's best features is that it never lies; it never tells tales, nor does it try to convince itself of how it feels. That job belongs to the mind, which spends most of its time trying to convince you that your heart is wrong, flawed, or too emotional to make decisions. The Eight of Cups is the heart's knowing. It knows when things are done, when to walk away, and that it can do so without needing to look back. At this point, the heart is ready to move on with love and let the lesson do the directing. Remove the Eight of Cups from your deck and place it somewhere you can see it. Then collect your journal and a pen: you are going to do some automatic writing from your heart.

If you feel so inclined, light a pink heart-colored candle and ask the Lady or her priestesses to hold space for you as you begin. Your writing will be centered around answering this question, which you should write at the top of your page: "What is it time to walk away from and why is it important to leave this energy behind?" Stare at your Eight of Cups card and take a few slow, deep, breaths as you let the question circulate around your head. Place your hands on your heart and steady yourself. Then pick up your pen and write whatever comes up; don't try and make sense of it or even try to use complete sentences. You can edit and fish through the content later. For now, all that matters is getting the message down on the page.

When you feel you are finished or that you can't seem to write anymore, put your pen down. Now find the Nine of Cups card and remove it from your deck. Place this card next to the Eight of Cups and turn to a clean page in your journal. While keeping the connection to your heart open, write the following question at the top of the page: "What is the dream my heart truly desires?" Once you have written the question, place your hands on your heart, and breathe slowly and deeply as you let the question repeat itself a few times in your head, then moving out into your third eye, and even further out into your aura.

Now pick up your pen and write. Again, do not try to make sense of what is being put on the paper; just get the words on the page. Write until there is nothing left—no pull from the heart, no words left in the energy. Put your pen down and place your hands on your heart one last time. Thank the Lady and her priestesses for being there with you if you called for them. Blow out your candle if you lit one, thanking the flame for being the light and guide for your words. Then say a general gratitude prayer either out loud or silently to close out your automatic writing session. You can place the cards back in your deck or move them to your altar.

If you feel so inclined, you can now look over what you have written. However, you do not have to review your writing straightaway—you can come back the following day because the time is irrelevant. When you do come back, see if you can create affirmations of intention statements out of the words.

These affirmations will amplify the work you have done with the cards. They will also help you make a connection to these two cards that perhaps you would not have made if you were only doing readings with them. Once you have your affirmations or intention statements, you can write them on notecards and keep them on your desk or your altar. What you do with the information you have gathered is entirely up to you.

Leaving the Circle and Moving On: Ten of Cups

Have you ever celebrated an ending? There is something very therapeutic about raising a glass and allowing yourself to party when something ends, and makes for a fantastic ritual to perform. Your time in the Temple of Cups has come to an end and the priestesses of Avalon are holding a feast in your honor, signifying the end of their teaching, healing, and clearing. Though the circle will open and the work is complete for now, this too is a form of initiation. The feast is the last thing you will do before leaving. You will celebrate and remind yourself that the future you are looking forward to is a result of the ending you now find yourself in the midst of. Here in the Temple of Cups, the ending is an emotional and healing one that will not just affect you but all those in your immediate circle. What you do when you leave this temple will have a lasting impact and set the tone of your legacy, which is why the High Priestess encourages you to celebrate now. Here you can acknowledge what you have accomplished, even if you don't quite know yet what that ending will bring you.

"Raise your cup, sister, and allow us to celebrate you and all you have done. Let us praise you and uplift your energy before you head forth into the future your heart desires." Cheers ring out through the forest as the Lady, eight priestesses, and you all drink deeply from your cups.

"Your heart has opened, little one, and you have listened to it. Take the steps to follow the path it has laid out for you." The Lady winks at you as she gets up to leave the feast. You understand your time here is done. For now, you will stay and revel with the priestesses.

Devotional Exercise

There is a time of the moon that is perfect for celebrating an ending, a phase that works hand in hand with the Lady's energy and all the dreams she wants you to manifest. That phase would be the waning crescent, the last phase before the new moon. This is where you celebrate your wins, release your failures, and give thanks to the goddess for all she has laid in your path. To start this moon ritual, you will need your Ten of Cups card from your deck. Place it on your altar. Next, write a gratitude or appreciation list that is extremely detailed. Don't just list things you are grateful for or appreciative of—explain why these things are important and how they have contributed to the success you are celebrating.

Once you have finished the list, place it on your altar together with the Ten of Cups. You will also need a birthday candle and a cupcake for this ritual. Remember—this is a cause for celebration, a way of honoring your blessings and lessons, so consider this your completion party. Place your candle in your cupcake and put both on your altar. Now light your candle and repeat the closing prayer:

Lady on High, bless this space

Energy of Avalon, see my success

We have come full circle

Bringing two ends together as one

Success is mine

Success is mine

Raise a cup, my priestess sisters

Celebrate this ending

For together we have created miracles

Letting go we move on

Success is mine

Success is mine

Planting seeds for futures to come

One cycle ends

Another begins

Raise a cup and celebrate with me

Success is mine

Success is mine

Lady on High

Take these words into your mist

Disperse them far and wide

For what is said is done

Now that your prayer is complete, blow out your candle and eat your cupcake. If you do not want to eat the whole thing, it is important to at least take a bite—ingesting your prayer and allowing it to nourish you is part of the ritual. Your time in the Temple of Cups is now complete. You can come back at any time to revisit the priestesses of Avalon and remind yourself of their lessons and healing. You can also call on the Lady at any time to invite her into your energy and ask her to guide you. She is always available, as are all the other goddesses mentioned in these pages. All you have to do is ask, trust, and receive.

CONCLUSION

〉〉●《《

When I first sat down to explore the idea for *Tarot Priestess*, I severely underestimated the complexity of the journey I was about to take. There is so much more I wanted to write, but it would have been overwhelming for those starting this journey for the very first time. We have covered a lot here: you have walked three gateways, explored the various stages of initiation, and worked at the feet of the goddess inside four temples. Each card has brought you a new lesson, a new message, and a new way of connecting to the Tarot Priestess path.

The path of the Tarot Priestess doesn't end here. If anything, the path is only beginning as your introduction to working with the tarot's seventy-eight cards in a deeper and more devotional way. It is up to you to decide where you would like to take this journey next. Will you keep this book by you at all times and use it as a way of connecting with the goddess daily through the act of bibliomancy? Will you set a tarot deck or two aside for your Tarot Priestess work? Maybe one of the biggest take-aways for you has been that you have been doing this priestess stuff all along but now you have a more refined, organized, and structured system to work with. Magic is amplified when it has order to it. The more focused and intentional we can be, the better the outcome. The real purpose of the work here was to show you how to order your priestess journey, giving you a set of protocols and principles that show you the path you have already been walking.

It matters not how you continue your journey, just that you do. Keep the door to the goddess open and welcome her into your daily life. Let her dance with you in celebration and bathe you in healing love during your more challenging moments. Use the teachings in this book to make mundane life magical. Breathe new life into your rituals and bring a deeper connection to your cards to your readings. All of these things will continue what we have started here. Personally, my mornings start with lighting a candle on my altar and giving thanks for all the goddess has bought into my life. I have tarot cards on my altar and allow them to set the vibrational energy of prayer as I set the tone of my day. Perhaps you will do something similar, or maybe now that you have made it to the end, you have crafted your own morning ritual.

Now is the time to come back to the Fool, the card you began with—the card that is *you*. It is time to stand on the cliff's edge of possibility once more, to get to know who you are now that you have finished your pilgrimage with this book. Stand with the Fool at the edge of the journey and see what magic has lined up for you to explore: Pull your Fool card from your deck and place it faceup in front of you. Pick up the rest of your deck and divide it into sections. Place all the major arcana cards in one pile, the court cards in another, and pull the four aces from the suits. Pick up your major arcana cards and shuffle them. Flip one over and place it next to your Fool card. Now pick up your court cards, shuffle them, flip one card over, and place it next to your major arcana card. Keeping the aces facedown so you can't see them, shuffle them and flip one over, and place it next to the court card. You will now have four cards:

CARD ONE: The Fool

CARD TWO: Major arcana / your gateway card

CARD THREE: Court card / your stage of initiation

CARD FOUR: Suits / your temple

These cards reveal the next journey, the seed the goddess has planted, the magic that awaits on the next phase of your Tarot Priestess journey. Having completed the exercises here, you know exactly what to do now and what work you need to do for yourself and your community. Just like the Fool, you will jump into this quest, this new pilgrimage, with both feet. You now know that the goddess is your safety net. The cards are your navigation system, and you are the master of your world.

Recommended Reading

)) ● ((

Bashford, Sophie. *You Are a Goddess: Working with the Sacred Feminine to Awaken, Heal, and Transform*. Carlsbad, CA: Hay House, 2018.

Blackie, Sharon. *If Women Rose Rooted: A Life-Changing Journey to Authenticity and Belonging*. Tewkesbury, UK: September Publishing, 2019.

Campbell, Rebecca. *Rise Sister, Rise: A Guide to Unleashing the Wise, Wild Woman Within*. London: Hay House, 2016.

Cousineau, Phil. *The Art of Pilgrimage: The Seeker's Guide to Making Travel Sacred*. San Francisco: Red Wheel/Weiser, 1998.

George, Demetra. *Mysteries of the Dark Moon: The Healing Power of the Dark Goddess*. New York: HarperCollins, 1992.

Goldberg, Dana. *Awaken Your Inner Goddess: Practical Tools for Self-Care, Emotional Healing, and Self-Realization*. Emeryville, CA: Rockridge Press, 2020.

Grimes, Ronald L. *Deeply into the Bone: Re-Inventing Rites of Passage*. Berkeley, CA: University of California Press, 2002.

Hunter, M. Kelley. *Living Lilith: Four Dimensions of the Cosmic Feminine.* Bournemouth, UK: The Wessex Astrologer, 2009.

Parker, Julie. *Priestess: Ancient Spiritual Wisdom for Modern Sacred Women.* Australia: the kind press, 2020.

Pollack, Rachel. *The Body of the Goddess: Sacred Wisdom in Myth, Landscape and Culture.* Dorset, UK: Element Books, 1997.

Reed, Theresa. *Astrology for Real Life: A Workbook for Beginners.* Newburyport, MA: Red Wheel/Weiser, 2019.

Telyndru, Jhenah. *The Mythic Moons of Avalon: Lunar and Herbal Wisdom from the Isle of Healing.* Woodbury, MN: Llewellyn Worldwide, 2020.

To Write to the Author

If you wish to contact the author or would like more information about this book, please write to the author in care of Llewellyn Worldwide Ltd. and we will forward your request. Both the author and publisher appreciate hearing from you and learning of your enjoyment of this book and how it has helped you. Llewellyn Worldwide Ltd. cannot guarantee that every letter written to the author can be answered, but all will be forwarded. Please write to:

Leeza Robertson
% Llewellyn Worldwide
2143 Wooddale Drive
Woodbury, MN 55125-2989

Please enclose a self-addressed stamped envelope for reply,
or $1.00 to cover costs. If outside the U.S.A., enclose
an international postal reply coupon.

Many of Llewellyn's authors have websites with additional information and resources. For more information, please visit our website at http://www.llewellyn.com